How Real Estate Professionals Can
Thrive in An Uncertain Future

Ian Morris, CEO, Market Leader

Steve Murray, editor, REAL *Trends*

Copyright © 2011 REAL *Trends*, Inc.
All rights reserved.

ISBN: **978-0-578-07904-2**

Art Direction and Design:
Travis Saxton, REAL *Trends*
and Chief Creative Image, LLC
Elizabeth, CO - Phone: 303-683-4815
www.tinyteegraphics.com - inside pages

Published by REAL *Trends*, Inc.
7501 Village Square Drive, Ste. 200
Castle Rock, CO 80108
Phone 303.741.1000

Advance Praise for *Game Plan*

"For those still confused and confounded by this perilous, unrelenting real estate market, Steve and Ian's new book provides not only clarity but great hope. Game Plan is factual, pragmatic, and unbiased, and I recommend it to everyone from crusty veterans to wide-eyed real estate rookies."

Marty Rueter, President
Weichert Real Estate Affiliates

"Not only did I read Game Plan, but I ordered it for my entire Leadership Team. This book by Morris/Murray provides a platform for all companies to creatively find their own road map for future sustainability and success."

Michael Saunders, founder & CEO
Michael Saunders & Company
Sarasota, Florida

"Game Plan provides insight and definition in a time of great change!"

Christopher J. Masiello, president & CEO
Better Homes and Gardens -The Masiello Group
Keene, New Hampshire

"This book gives detailed insight into the forces shaping the future of our industry while providing interesting historical context of how we ended up where we are today. It is a must-read for anyone that plans to thrive in real estate into the future."

Eric Thompson, president
The Group Real Estate
Fort Collins, Colorado

It's never easy and it's never clear
who's to navigate and who's to steer;

And so we flounder
drifting ever near the rocks.

Dan Fogelberg
The Innocent Age

Dedication

To my parents, for doing everything right
and making everything possible.

To my children Hannah, Kaylee, and Robbie,
for filling every moment with joy.

To my lovely wife Lisa, for somehow keeping it all together
and putting up with me every day.

I am truly blessed.

~ Ian ~

For the people who matter most to me:
T., Brian and Cooper

~ Steve ~

Special Thanks

No project of this kind is due to one person. The REAL *Trends* team including Doniece Welch, Amy Broset, Nicolai Kolding, Travis Saxton, Daniele Stufft and Tracey Velt were invaluable with their comments and recommendations that made this a far better book. Thanks for being part of the best team in the business.

Special thanks to Anne Murray Randolph for her excellent work on housing and consumers. No one in or out of our business knows the topic better.

Matt Heinz of Heinz Marketing, Michael and Ellie Sheldon at XMedia Communications, and Danae Hordyk and Brandy Wyckoff-Murphy at Market Leader also provided instrumental assistance in making *Game Plan* a reality.

Dozens of industry leaders provided access to their time and thoughts about the future and, for this, we are sincerely thankful. Without their willingness to share, there would be no *Game Plan* for the future.

Learn more at
www.realestategameplan.com

Table of Contents

Table of Contents

Table of Contents

Introduction

For most of the last 30 years, there's been a feeling of insecurity among real estate professionals. Will buyers and sellers forgo the use of our services and buy and sell without us? Will the Internet enable them to do so? Will some outside force intrude in our business, steal our relationships and cut into our incomes?

Behind the scenes—and in some cases, out in the open—these discussions have been going on for the last 30 years. There's always another threat looming over the horizon: Some monstrous outside force, perhaps new forms of government regulation, a change in the mortgage interest deduction or some other change in the legal environment that will erode the business of brokerage. Big banks could wreak havoc or a technology behemoth might rip our customers away.

While the types of threats and the level of them have changed over the years, the feeling that disaster is just around the corner has been a part of the DNA of the residential brokerage industry throughout the modern age.

Perhaps it's the perception that the money is too good, the level of effort too low or the requirements too easy for real estate professionals to make a living. While paranoia is too strong a word, an underlying sense of unease permeates the profession.

Either the market is overheated or else it's weak; mortgage rates too high or financing difficult. Every slight ripple in the environment seems to bring out the concern that real estate as we have known it is coming to an end.

Yet consumers continue to use real estate professionals at virtually the same rate, for the same terms, and requiring nearly the same services, as they have for the last 30 years. Yes, the means by which professionals reach and communicate with clients has changed. The forms required for selling and buying are vastly more numerous and complicated, but it's just more paperwork and doesn't represent any change to the foundation of how homes are bought and sold.

Changes to the way real estate transactions happen are much less drastic than, for instance, the way buying stocks, books, music and airline tickets have changed.

Why has real estate brokerage survived the onslaught of these outside forces for so long?

Simply put, there's too much at stake in the purchase of a home for most consumers to go it alone. Mike Staver, an organizational behaviorist says that the number one motivating factor for humans is the "avoidance of pain."

Lorne Wallace, CEO of Lone Wolf, a real estate technology firm, says, "The cost of failure in anything we purchase or decisions we make is a huge factor. The cost of failure in buying or selling a home is huge relative to the cost of failure in buying a book, a plane ticket or a song."

Joel Singer, CEO of the California Association of Realtors, adds, "One has to remember that the purchase or sale of a home is both an infrequent transaction and a highly complex one. Consumers are not familiar with the steps in a purchase or sale and, thus far, see their real estate professional as a consultant to help them through the process and avoid failure."

The avoidance of pain and the fear of failure clearly play an important role in why consumers have used real estate professionals in the past and will continue to do so in the future.

The sales relationship will stay the same as long as real estate professionals continue to provide real world benefits to their customers. What has changed is the demographic profile of today's homebuyers. We are no longer serving a population that is so predominantly white, male, married with children, professional and so forth. And the type of housing desired by these new generations of consumers is evolving as well.

At the same time, the economic underpinnings of the housing market have changed irrevocably since the downturn in housing and start of the great recession. We can no longer count on house prices increasing, with only an occasional pause as the market takes a breather. The recession destroyed almost half the wealth of the Baby Boomers, and seriously interfered with the employment prospects of the younger generations.

To add another level of complexity, government regulations make it harder to lend to less-qualified buyers. In a word, today's homebuyers are much less flush than the consumers we've grown accustomed to serving.

Taken together, these factors—heightened competition, technological upheaval, demographic change, and a new economic reality—mean we will have to work harder, adapt more quickly, learn new skills, and consistently apply best practices, if we are to succeed.

And that is our goal in this book. *Game Plan* begins with a series of chapters that examine how we got to our current situation. It examines the disruptive factors that have buffeted our industry:

1. *New Business Models and the Changing Economics of Brokerage*
2. *The Arrival of the Internet*
3. *Changing Demographics and Economic Upheaval*

These disruptions have redefined our industry in recent years and helped shape the four distinct business models that are most prominent today. We'll look at the historical development and economic characteristics of these models and what they mean to us as we try to master the economic, technological and demographic realities that will shape our future.

We will then outline each of the ten trends that we believe will drive our industry over the next five years.

Finally, and perhaps most importantly, we will outline the strategies – our game plans – for success in this environment. We do this with two distinct game plans, one for brokerage firms and one for real estate professionals. Both are focused on building practical, actionable strategies for success for those who are focused on building successful, profitable, and durable real estate businesses for the years to come.

We hope that you find *Game Plan* to be beneficial and that you enjoy the journey.

Chapter 1

The Challenge of Predicting the Future

~~~~~~~~~~~~~~~~~~~~~~~~~~~~~

We may never know about the days to come.
But we think about them anyway.

~~~~~~~~~~~~~~~~~~~~~~~~~~~~~

Carly Simon – Anticipation

Every business leader struggles with divining the future. As former Secretary of Defense Donald Rumsfeld put it, "there are just too many unknown unknowns." We don't know what we don't know.

The leaders of residential brokerages are no different. Numerous times in the past thirty years, trends and threats that many thought would have a major impact did not play out the way most thought they would.

The fact that even the most knowledgeable, business-savvy people of their day could not make accurate predictions about the direction of their industry has to make us all pause and reflect on what really is the highest and best use of our time at work.

The time is October, 1981. A group of leading independent brokerage firms who were associated with a national referral network called InterCommunity Relocation (ICR) met for a two-day strategic planning session. The goal was to discuss the landscape for residential brokerage, the future of their firms and of the network that had been formed in 1971. Among those present were the leaders of Edina Realty, Long and Foster, DeWolfe, Baird and Warner, Van Schaack and

Grubb & Ellis— all, at that time, among the top firms in their markets. The environment for housing sales, for brokerage firms and for the ICR network was decidedly chilly. Housing sales had collapsed since 1979 and were off over 40 percent from the peak in 1979. Interest rates were in the high teens. Merrill Lynch Realty had entered the industry in late 1977 and had already bought several members of the ICR network. Sears was buying Coldwell Banker. Homequity had formed its own referral network and several other members of ICR had decamped.

So these leaders were faced with peril on all sides. Declining housing sales were making their businesses unprofitable just as new, formidable national brokerage firms were chipping away at their firms and their network. To say that those present were concerned, would be an understatement.

After two days of discussions and analysis, the general agreement was that the housing market and economy would recover in time, that interest rates would subside and that consumers were still inclined to own their own homes. For the core business of their firms, the recession would pass and sales would recover.

The threat posed by Merrill Lynch Realty and the Sears/Coldwell Banker combination was another matter. Not only were they buying and building their realty businesses, but they were causing the loss of significant membership in the ICR network and many felt that their ability to access capital might enable them to become far stronger competitors than had ever been seen before in residential brokerage. Plans were discussed and strategies agreed upon to deal with these clear and present dangers.

Interestingly, one relatively new organization was discussed briefly, but then quickly dismissed as not much of a competitive threat. The newfangled business model—paying sales people 100 percent commission—did not make much sense. And, a small national franchise, based in Denver, was not viewed as having the size or staying power to escape the recession. Surely their early gains would be erased once the market recovered.

That firm, RE/MAX, grew to be the largest residential franchise in terms of sales within the next 15 years.

In fact, it didn't take very long for the RE/MAX business model to impact leading traditional brokerage firms. Within three to four years nearly every incumbent brokerage firm would see significant losses of their top sales professionals to the new upstart. By the end of the 1980s, most traditional firms were offering their own 100 percent commission plans in an attempt to slow or stop the loss of top-producing sales professionals.

And what of the threat posed by Merrill Lynch Realty and Sears/ Coldwell Banker? Merrill Lynch Realty was sold to Prudential Real Estate Affiliates in 1989. Sears sold Coldwell Banker Residential to a private investment group in 1992. It turned out that the residential brokerage business was far more challenging than either had thought. The business of selling homes was far different than security sales or retailing. And the financial returns were far less than the leaders of Merrill Lynch and Sears predicted when their firms entered the business.

In hindsight, it's easy enough to formulate the lessons learned from this episode:

- Disruptions in competitive markets frequently come from within an industry, not outside; and from below, not above.

- New forms of competition do not have to be large (or have a large market share) to cause significant disruption to the incumbents' businesses.

- Disruptive innovations don't have to be technological. RE/MAX created a novel compensation structure to corral the best sales people—and those sales people brought their customers with them.

◆ Predicting The Future Is Difficult

The failure of leadership to accurately forecast where the real threats are is legend—regardless of the type of business or whether the organization is private or public. Today, basing the survival of the enterprise on leadership's ability to accurately depict where and how markets and businesses will move, is a strategy fraught with peril, particularly for incumbents in any field.

If you are still in doubt, here are a few more examples taken from our own industry of experts who were unable to get it right—despite their undoubted expertise and good intentions.

In a speech to the leadership of the National Association of Realtors®, then NAR President, Bill Chee, warned of "the lion coming over the hill." While he was correct in saying that information giants and the advent of the Internet would impact the industry, it turns out that even when consumers gained access to this information they didn't change the manner in which they buy and sell homes. The percentage of consumers using Realtors® has stayed steady since listing information became widely available. And despite the investment of hundreds of millions of dollars by outside entities to 'change' or 'reform' brokerage, the means and methods by which real estate professionals provide service remains very much like it was before the Internet.

In early 1995, a firm, then known as Hospitality Franchise Systems (HFS), surprised everyone when it bought the CENTURY 21 franchise system. Then, with subsequent purchases of ERA, Coldwell Banker and PHH (owner of Homequity), the firm today, known as Realogy, assembled the largest set of residential brokerage assets ever seen. No one had ever owned and operated more than one brand; today Realogy has six.

Also, no one had ever approached the share of market in both brokerage and relocation management that Realogy built. No one had predicted that this level of consolidation could ever occur, except, of course, the people at Realogy who made it happen.

From a start in 1987, Keller Williams Realty International grew slowly for its first 10 years or so. As was the case with RE/MAX in its early years, virtually every incumbent ignored the threat that Keller Williams posed to their business. By the early 2000s, Keller Williams was among the fastest-growing realty organizations in the country and brokerage firms were scrambling to build both their offenses and defenses against this new, aggressive competitor.

Perhaps the most glaring evidence of the failure to accurately forecast the future in housing and brokerage, was the inability of any leaders to forecast the depth of the housing downturn that started in the middle of the last decade and continues to this day.

Over the last five years, we've experienced the longest, deepest housing downturn in 80 years and no one in a leadership position, private sector or public, knew how deep and devastating it would be. Yes, there were a few financial analysts who, in 2003, were discussing the potential, but their voices were drowned out by those with more 'experience.'

◆ Why Is It So Difficult To Predict The Future?

There are several reasons leaders fail to predict the future. Here are a few.

1. Most leaders can only see what's in front of them.

They're good at measuring demand for their product given 'x' employment rates, 'y' interest rates, and 'z' spending patterns. This is true for any organization. The focus is mostly on the here and now, or the near-term future.

Most leaders in housing knew that housing moves in cycles and, likewise, knew an adjustment was coming in 2004-2005. What they didn't want to believe was the data that indicated just how far the market was out of sync with fundamentals. Every organization involved in the housing business assumed that a downturn would be short, just like in the past. Very few economic indicators pointed to anything other than a return-to-normal housing market. Clearly, leadership didn't look as closely as they should have.

What do you imagine was on the minds of the leaders of firms like Digital Equipment Corporation, Wang Computer, and IBM when Microsoft, Apple and Intel first appeared?

2.   Changes take place over time and there will always be time to adjust.

Also known by the "boiling the frog" theory where a frog will jump out of water that's already hot; but, sit patiently and get boiled when the heat is turned up over time.

Change does occur but usually over long periods of time. Thus, there's a concurrent belief that whatever major structural or strategic changes may be taking place can be responded to in time to head off major business impacts.

RE/MAX was nearly 10 years old before they began to have an impact nationally. The same was true of Keller Williams. Incumbent brokerage firms just didn't believe that their sales professionals would leave for these new value propositions. They thought sales professionals who had been with them for years just wouldn't do that. Or, they imagined that anyone who had defected would surely return when the market returned to normal.

Southwest Airlines began operating in the early 1970s. Yet even when the major airlines (United, American, Delta, and Northwest) knew that discount airlines were growing, they still put off any changes to their business models believing that their customers were 'different' and, their established hub-and-spoke systems and frequent-flyer programs would enable them to hold onto their customers. Bankruptcy followed for almost every one of them.

Sam Walton founded Walmart in the mid-1960s. What was the

reaction of Sears, JCPenney, Kmart and Montgomery Ward? For nearly 20 years, absolutely nothing. They assumed their customers were not interested in the Walmart offering and even if there were shifts in buying patterns, they could react in time. Walmart today is nearly 10 times larger than the other four *combined.*

MCI entered business in the early 1970s. It must have seemed insane to think they could compete with the largest monopoly in the United States at the time, AT&T. This alternative introduced a new way of seeing the market, and, by 1984, AT&T was broken up into regional phone operating companies, with only the long distance business retaining the AT&T identity.

What many fail to understand is how new products, services and business models develop—and how fast they can spread. Malcolm Gladwell, in his book, *The Tipping Point* says, "the best way to understand the emergence of fashion trends, the ebb and flow of crime waves or the transformation of an unknown book into a best seller is to think of them as epidemics. Ideas and messages and behaviors spread just like viruses do." New business models, like viruses, spread slowly at first but by the time they impact the body (the market), the patient is likely quite ill.

In the cases of RE/MAX and Keller Williams, it took a fairly long period of time for the "virus" of their new way of doing business to propagate. But once that happened, they spread rapidly. Neither RE/MAX nor Keller Williams had more than 2 percent market share nationally when the impact of their new business models began to affect the way traditional brokerage firms had to operate.

Gladwell sums it up by saying, "We need to prepare ourselves for the possibility that sometimes big changes follow from small events."

3. Hubris

We are generally dismissive of those who are different.
We don't often heed the signals that the fundamentals are changing.

Earl Lee, CEO,
Prudential Real Estate Affiliates
Irvine, California

Nothing can be as deadly as thinking the way we have always done things will always work. This pattern of thought is called 'hubris.' and it's the mirror image of the phenomenon we examined in the previous section. There, business leaders felt they could safely ignore upstart competitors who were small—because there would always be time to adjust. 'Hubris' is thinking you are so big and important, the market can't afford to ignore you.

Incumbents are particularly prone to hubris. This is also true of organizations and people who have been leaders in their market segments or businesses for a long period. Hubris leads these leaders to consider themselves invincible. In residential brokerage, it would be good to ask firms such as Gallery of Homes and Homes For Living how things worked out for them when CENTURY 21, RE/MAX and ERA were all launched in the early 1970s.

The incumbents in brokerage were seriously disrupted when, first, RE/MAX and, then, Keller Williams entered the market. Unlike the launches of Coldwell Banker and Prudential, which built their systems with mainly the traditional graduated commission plan model, RE/MAX and Keller Williams were entirely new forms of realty companies with different ways of doing business. They also relied mostly on start-up franchises instead of existing brokerage firms. Not only were they young and small, their 'funny' way of doing business was disregarded by many as unethical, low brow or cultish. Likely Sears, United Airlines, IBM and others felt the same way just before another company came along and wrecked either their economics, or their entire business model.

Philip Evans wrote in *Blown to Bits* that, "the most venerable can prove the most vulnerable. The history, the myths, the shared values and the unreflective presuppositions that define a strong corporate culture can blind business leaders to events that do not fit into their collective mental framework."

Put another way, leaders of all kinds of businesses become strongly attached to what they've built over time to the extent that they're captive to group think. They've surrounded themselves with people who agree with them and support their worldview.

It's a difficult balancing act. Often, successful companies have been built on fundamentals that never go out of style, such as, a focus on building a strong culture, being open and transparent with your team and delivering consistently good quality customer service. However, in order to stay relevant, an incumbent firm must learn new ways to talk about and deliver these fundamentals. Aspects of the business may need to change entirely when there are new, competitive products or services on the landscape. This is especially true of new business models that are more efficient, particularly for the consumer.

The key is to understand that it is really the fundamental values that are essential to success, rather than any particular product, service, or prediction about the market.

Remember the leaders we talked about above, the ones whose predictions were so far off base? They were the best and brightest and most experienced in their field. And, in most cases, they couldn't have been more wrong. That's a sobering lesson. It reminds us to focus our efforts on things we can control: The kind of people we hire, the way we treat our customers, the quality of our service, and the integrity of our industry. That way, we have a solid foundation, regardless of how the markets behave.

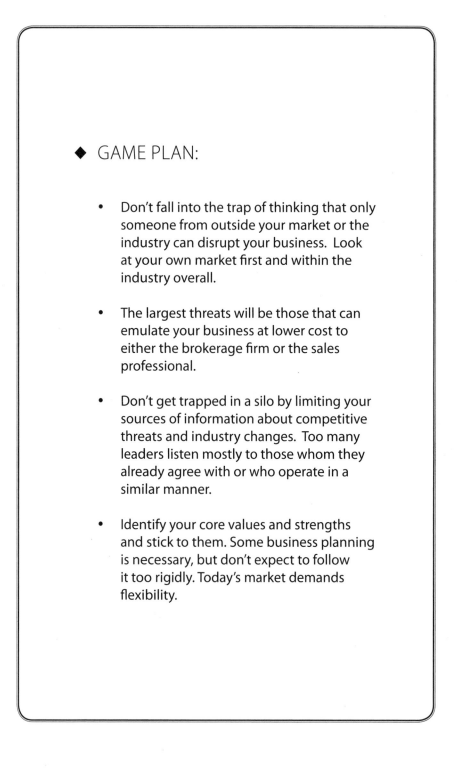

◆ GAME PLAN:

- Don't fall into the trap of thinking that only someone from outside your market or the industry can disrupt your business. Look at your own market first and within the industry overall.

- The largest threats will be those that can emulate your business at lower cost to either the brokerage firm or the sales professional.

- Don't get trapped in a silo by limiting your sources of information about competitive threats and industry changes. Too many leaders listen mostly to those whom they already agree with or who operate in a similar manner.

- Identify your core values and strengths and stick to them. Some business planning is necessary, but don't expect to follow it too rigidly. Today's market demands flexibility.

Chapter 2

The Modern Brokerage Industry

The first of the major forces that disrupted the status quo in the residential real estate brokerage industry was the advent of new business models.

This chapter provides a historical perspective that intertwines the story of those models with that of other forces, such as technology, to provide a sense of how things unfolded over time.

Understanding how brokerage firms evolved—and what decisions and forces brought them to this point—can aid leaders in determining where to move next, where to invest, and how to successfully structure their firms for the future.

This chapter also introduces one of the most important trends that you will see throughout this book: How our industry evolved from a firm-centric to a professional-centric model. We will then look at recent indications of a new transition to a lead-centric model as the importance of lead generation gains traction in our industry.

◆ Today's Brokerage Firm

*I understand that technology will change the way business is done.
But I had a record year last year; in fact,
I have had 10 consecutive record years in growth
of profits from my brokerage.*

*Now while I understand that the business will change,
I've also been hearing that from every corner of the industry
for the last 10 to 15 years. There's simply no way, at my age,
that I'm going to turn my business inside out to accommodate
the changes that 'experts' think are required to succeed in the future.
That is for the next generation.*

CEO of one of REAL *Trends'* top 25 brokerage companies
Spring 2006

This statement, from a highly respected leader of a traditional
brokerage firm, aptly sums up the prevailing view of the vast majority
of owners of the nation's leading residential brokerage firms. Many of
these leaders started their careers in brokerage as sales professionals.
Some moved up the ranks within their firm; others started their own
firms or acquired existing firms.

Over the past 30 years, brokerage firm owners have survived a series
of what we, only half-jokingly, call apocalyptic events. These include
four housing downturns, the first entry of publicly held firms into
brokerage, the disruption of traditional business practices by new
models, and the opening of the MLS to the public. No wonder the
current generation of owners doesn't feel threatened by the vast
potential for change in the way consumers use brokerage to buy and
sell homes today.

Adequately meeting the future requires that we understand the past.
In other words:

- How did brokerage firms develop as they have?

- Why are some affiliated with national brands while others are not?
- Why do firms operate the way they do—and what stops them from changing their business model?
- What are the characteristics of the most successful firms—and what do these tell us about how brokerage firms will adapt and thrive in the times ahead?

◆ The Beginning Of The Modern Age Of Brokerage

The entry of Merrill Lynch into the realty business in the fall of 1977 marked the beginning of what we call 'the modern age' of the brokerage business. While CENTURY 21, RE/MAX and ERA were all founded before this time, the entry of Merrill Lynch (and to some extent, Meredith Corporation and its Better Homes and Gardens Real Estate franchise) was different. These were the first of several large, well-capitalized firms that would enter the residential brokerage business over the next four decades. By contrast, CENTURY 21, RE/MAX and ERA were private start-ups, mainly run by real estate entrepreneurs.

Merrill Lynch's stated aim was to create a one-stop shopping experience for customers. Through its ownership of residential brokerage firms, it could integrate all services and products related to the purchase and sale of housing. To all appearances, Merrill had the capital, technology and clout on Wall Street to achieve its goals.

When Merrill was making its moves, two other changes were occurring in brokerage that would have profound and long-lasting effects. The first was the surrender of the Realtor® organization on the issue of the solicitation of sales professionals. Until that point, it was against the Code of Ethics of the National Association of Realtors® (NAR) for a one-member firm to solicit another member's sales professionals.

The second change was the rise of the modern relocation management firm. This was the first time outside firms inserted themselves between a brokerage firm and its sales professionals on the one hand, and the purchasers and sellers of homes on the other.

The ability of one firm to solicit another firm's professionals was akin to the changes brought to major league sports with the advent of free agency. This change ushered in what many refer to as the professional-centric age of real estate brokerage.

While real estate professionals have always had the right to move from one firm to another, it previously occurred far less than it has since this change took place in the late 1970s. Firms could now aggressively pursue other firms' sales professionals rather than rely on developing their own. Sales professionals used their newfound freedoms to begin the now decades-old practice of seeking higher returns for their "book of business." The impact of this change continues to be felt today.

The entry of relocation management firms into residential brokerage was more subtle. At first, the leading relocation management businesses of the time, including Merrill Lynch, Homequity, Equitable, Executrans and Employee Transfer Corporation, were content to share the action. They would use brokerage firms for the valuation, acquisition, management and resale of properties, and to assist families with finding homes in their new locations.

With the entry of Merrill Lynch into the realty business, its relocation business began leveraging its existing customer base to build networks of affiliated brokerage firms. Homequity formed its brokerage business in 1979, Coldwell Banker in 1981 and Equitable in 1983. Many leading firms of that time opted to either sell to Merrill Lynch or affiliate with a national relocation management referral network.

They did so because during the downturn of the early 1980s, corporate relocation assignments were a high-value business for any firm. Even though no single relocation management firm controlled even one quarter of one percent of the national housing market, the networks they created during this time would form the basis for some of the strongest networks today. Two of them (Merrill Lynch and Coldwell Banker) would use their volumes of relocation management business to build strong franchise brands (Merrill Lynch was acquired by

Prudential Real Estate Affiliates in 1989). Thus, relatively small amounts of actual business were leveraged to create leading national brands.

The subsequent acquisition of Coldwell Banker by Sears in 1981 amplified the impact of these changes. By 1981, Sears/Coldwell Banker and Merrill Lynch Realty were considered grave threats to the incumbent traditional brokerage firms of that time. The entry of these two firms also inspired their two biggest competitors in relocation management, Homequity and Equitable, to build their own networks of affiliated brokerage firms. Homequity formalized and broadened the financial and operational requirements for brokerages to join their network and get their assignments. Equitable acquired one of the largest networks of independent brokerage firms, renaming it and increasing the financial yields through this new relationship.

The entry of these firms was just the beginning of an onslaught of change. The recession of 1981-82, the opportunity for firms to recruit sales professionals from competitors, the advance of the 100 percent commission concept, and the creation of new networks built around outside sources of business all contributed to the brokerage industry that operates today. The traditional brokerage firms that had dominated the industry until this point were assailed on all sides. For the first time, they faced competition based on the commission structures they offered their sales professionals—and from large, well-capitalized entries into their market.

It's important to understand scale at this time as well. Less than a handful of firms had more than 500 sales professionals and the number of firms that did more than 5,000 transactions per year was equally small. Mortgage and other core service revenues were virtually non-existent. These multiple threats were seen, not as passing issues, but as potentially life threatening.

◆ The Advent Of The 'Professional-Centric' Industry

For brokerages, the answer to these challenges was to beef up their ranks. They grew their sales professional population, increased the size of their retail network of branch offices, and increased the size of each branch office to accommodate a wider range of sales professional productivity. If the revenue yield to the brokerage was going to be less for each professional, then one obvious response was *more sales professionals*.

A majority of the leading residential brokerage firms embraced this strategy regardless of their location or affiliation. And for the past 30 years, this has been the core strategy of virtually every leading residential brokerage in the industry. One result was larger firms with more sales professionals—albeit with lower per-person productivity (as shown below).

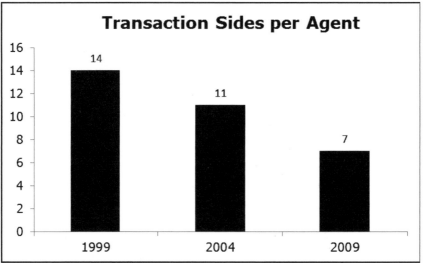

Source: REAL *Trends* 500 and Up-and-Comers, 2010

Along the way, the firms that grew the most and had the highest gross profits were the firms that sought to add sales professionals to their roster. They also, for the most part, attempted to retain them without regard to their sales production.

RE/MAX, and a few other firms, focused more on highly productive professionals for most of this time. And, to some extent, the majority of leading firms have been pursuing this strategy for the last decade.

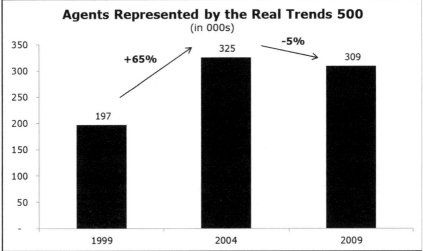

Source: REAL *Trends* 500 and Up-and-Comers, 2010

Brokerage firms had choices. A firm could pursue the strategy of growing its professional force without regard to productivity; or, it could stay focused on retaining only high-producing sales professionals. Since the number of high producers is a relatively small percentage of all sales professionals, it was widely believed that pursuing the latter would relegate a brokerage firm to permanently smaller market share. With the RE/MAX system garnering a relatively large share of these professionals—and at a high cost—it was believed that such a firm would have lower profits as well.

For the past 30 years, this was probably the right strategy for a majority of the largest firms. From 1985 to 2005 the leading traditional brokerage firms, regardless of brand affiliation, grew their share of all sales professionals and grew their share of total transactions and sales volumes. While their brokerage profit margins continued to be under pressure from increasing payments to sales professionals, the incorporation of mortgage, title insurance and other settlement service–related revenues into their businesses, more than made up the difference.

During the bull market that ran from the early 1990s to 2006, total gross profits for these volume-minded firms soared. While commission levels declined, they did so more slowly than the average price of the homes being sold. And for most firms, the growth in revenue per transaction grew faster than the cost of operations. Added to gross profits from core services, the professional-centric model was a bonanza for both brokerage firms and their sales professionals from 1985 to 2006.

There were exceptions to this trend. Many RE/MAX firms achieved high market share in dozens of U.S. markets from 1990-2005. Independent firms such as The Group Inc. in Fort Collins, Colorado; and The Kentwood Company in Denver, achieved high market shares while focusing solely on the recruitment and retention of only highly productive sales professionals. There are several smaller firms across the country that achieved similar results in smaller markets. As a general rule, however, these types of firms did not achieve either the net profit margins or total gross profits of their larger peers.

Through 2006, regardless of the advent of the Internet and the entry of dozens of technology-based realty offerings, the large professional-centric firms continued to dominate the residential brokerage industry.

◆ The Explosive Growth Of National Brands

Being associated with a well-known, reputable, nationally-branded, real estate organization is highly important to most productive sales professionals. While technology, education and lead generation are also key, a strong brand matters as well.

Dave Liniger, chairman - RE/MAX LLC
Denver, Colorado

At the start of the modern age in 1977, there were three identifiable national franchises with only one, CENTURY 21, having a true national footprint. RE/MAX, ERA, Realty Executives and Realty World were in business, but had little market presence on a national basis at that time. CENTURY 21 was far and away the dominant national firm.

1977 marked the entrance of the original Better Homes and Gardens affiliation. Coldwell Banker launched its franchise in 1982, followed by Prudential and Keller Williams in 1987.

By 1990, these nationally-branded networks had 32 percent market share of all professionally-assisted transactions. By 2009, their combined share had grown to 48 percent. Even more remarkably, 84 percent of all of the firms on the REAL *Trends 500* and *Up-and-Comers* rankings are affiliated with a national brand, up from 58 percent in 1990. Today, branded network affiliations truly rule the roost in the brokerage business.

These networks evolved in different ways. CENTURY 21, ERA, Realty World, Realty Executives and RE/MAX began as privately funded start-ups and were built through the sale of master franchise territories to other private capital sources, and through direct franchise sales.

None of the above firms had connections to existing relocation management firms that would have been a source of business leads; nor, did these early franchised networks have access to capital to loan to, or invest in, brokerage firm acquisitions or to fund growth internally. Keller Williams, a later entrant, was privately held and also grew through the private sale of territories to private investors.

The original Better Homes and Gardens, Coldwell Banker and Prudential Real Estate affiliates went a different route. They were backed by capital from significant publicly held parent corporations and each also owned or controlled sizeable relocation management businesses. Other than outside the United States, they did not sell master franchises. They were effective in growing their brands through a combination of capital and leveraging their existing relocation management operations.

Coldwell Banker combined franchising with corporate ownership of brokerage firms in several markets around the country. By the late 1980s, however, the firm began to sell many of its corporately owned and operated brokerage firms to other entities that became franchises of Coldwell Banker.

Prudential started as a purely franchising organization. After its acquisition of the former Merrill Lynch Realty and Relocation businesses, Prudential provided financing as well when these operations were sold—in many cases, back to the original owners who had originally sold them to Merrill Lynch.

Along with picking up many large brokerage firms as new franchises, Prudential owned the second-largest relocation management business in the United States at that time.

RE/MAX, Keller Williams and Realty Executives all offered a distinctive business model for franchisees. RE/MAX and Realty Executives focused on high-commission offerings to attract sales professionals. Keller Williams structured a business model for both broker/owners and sales professionals that included unique sales commission splits and a profit-sharing program. (We've simplified each firm's offerings here for the purposes of comparison.)

With the entry of HFS (today known as Realogy) into residential brokerage, the branded network achieved yet another milestone. Through the acquisition, first of CENTURY 21, followed by ERA and Coldwell Banker, one firm now controlled brand-name franchises that accounted for close to 20 percent of all transactions handled by brokerage firms in the United States.

In a related investment, HFS acquired PHH Corporation, a large relocation management and mortgage-banking firm. With this additional acquisition, HFS achieved the leadership position in brokerage and relocation management.

One other attribute separates the way these firms grew. Keller Williams, Realty Executives and RE/MAX expanded through franchising start-up firms based on their unique operating models. Their competitors almost always sold franchises to existing, more traditional, brokerage firms, which then transformed themselves to align with the national brand.

What helped to spur the significant growth of the nationally-branded networks, from the late 1980s to the present, was the attraction these brands held for both businesses and consumers. Many brokerage firms believed that national brand identity was a significant plus. Most firms offered a wide range of marketing, training and education programs that were difficult for smaller, local brokerage firms to replicate.

Additionally, in the case of RE/MAX, Realty Executives and Keller Williams, each brand offered a distinctive business model and value proposition for sales professionals. For Prudential and Realogy, there were substantial relocation and affinity management assignments. And these two firms also offered capital in several forms to assist their franchisees in expansion through mergers and acquisitions.

Ultimately, no one reason can explain the collective growth of the national brands. What did become apparent during these years of rapid growth was that the larger traditional firms typically remained independent. Other than through acquisitions, the larger regional and local firms chose to stay with their own brands and depended on their own resources to compete.

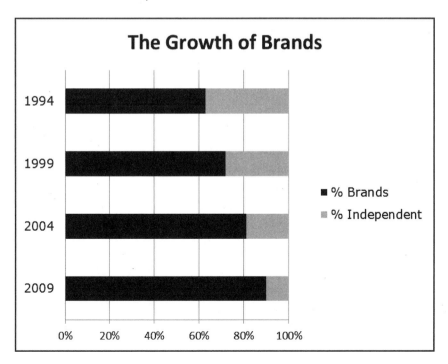

◆ The Internet Arrives

The Internet and its presence in residential brokerage first became an issue in the fall of 1995. At the NAR convention, a NAR subsidiary, Realtor Information Network (RIN), offered to assist professionals and brokerage firms with the placement and management of their listings online. While several brokerage firms already had their listings online, these efforts were neither widespread nor sophisticated—at least by today's standards. As a major focal point of the 1995 NAR convention, the RIN effort attracted a great deal of attention.

Brokerage firms and professionals became aware of just how fast moving this new environment would be when, within the space of a weekend in Atlanta, the cost of placing a listing online went from over $2 per listing to essentially zero. RIN's offer was trumped in the space of two days by more aggressive, lower-cost competitors. This was the first indication that the Internet would have a profound impact on how residential brokerage information would be distributed.

At that time, NAR, the national networks, brokerage firms, sales professionals and most related parties had yet 'to take a stance' on the Internet. It took nearly a decade before rules and policies related to the use of the web—most particularly how, when and where listings could be shown online—would be formalized.

During this time period, brokerage firms and their sales professionals began displaying their listings wherever there were potential consumers looking for information about housing. There are several hundred thousand sites that contain some information about listings, sales, neighborhoods and more. As in many other industries, there are a few sites that have a relatively large viewership. However, when one looks at the total of all housing-market viewers on the Internet, the market remains a highly-fragmented one.

*One thing that has changed and will continue to evolve
is that housing consumers don't seek a trusted adviser first…
they trust the 'machine' first.*

Dan Elsea, president - Real Estate One
Detroit, Michigan

What's most intriguing about the 1995-2011 period is how little
change this powerful new tool created in the practice of brokerage
or the operations of brokerage firms. While 85-90 percent of all
consumers start their search for property online, the percentage of
those using a real estate sales professional to assist with either selling
or buying a home has remained relatively equal to the percentage
found prior to the web's becoming an everyday presence in residential
real estate. This has confounded many technology-oriented
businesses—but not most brokerage firms and sales professionals.
As we discuss in more depth in our chapter on technology, buying a
home is a complex pursuit, and the Internet can only go so far in terms
of replicating the expertise—and the experience—to be gained by
working personally with a sales professional.

Research from Realtor.com, in the fall of 2010, indicates that the
percentage of those who found online the home they ultimately
bought now exceeds those that found it through a sales professional.
The same research indicates that the percentage of consumers who
found their sales professional online has climbed from less than 1
percent 10 years ago, to over 15 percent today. This is not surprising,
as most consumers begin their search online—and many seek advice
through social media sites. What's also true is that *the percentage
of consumers who find their real estate professional through personal
knowledge or referral has remained virtually unchanged in the last 30
years or so.*

The bottom line is that there's been little to no shift in the market
shares of firms or national networks due to the entry and impact of the
web. While certain firms, such as ZipRealty and Redfin, have gained
share in certain markets, their overall influence has been negligible
thus far. The largest brokerage firms and national networks have

adopted many of the web strategies pioneered by upstarts. These tactics have blunted any advantage the Internet-focused companies may have gained, despite, in some cases, having superior technology.

The Internet has had a profound effect on the level of information that consumers have access to about housing and has increased their leverage with sales professionals. Nonetheless, it has not had an impact in terms of reduced use of professionals, nor in the commissions or fees that consumers pay for their services. In other words, an "Internet revolution" has not occurred in residential real estate—at least to the degree of magnitude that it has in many other industries.

◆ The Emphasis On Lead Generation

The impact of the Internet has perhaps been felt most in the growth of lead generation. What *has* changed is the new emphasis, by leading networks and brokerage firms as well as some technology and media upstarts, on using their web presence to drive consumers to sales professionals affiliated with their companies. Of course national networks, brokerage firms and sales professionals have always focused on generating phone calls and emails—that's what advertising expenditures are all about. The web's difference is in the opportunity it provides to measure the effectiveness of advertising (whether traditional or online), and to build business systems and rules in an attempt to capture these opportunities more effectively.

The ability of networks and brokerage firms to increase lead generation is similar to the importance of leveraging a relocation management business in the past. Both the networks and brokerage firms tout their effectiveness online. The number of unique visitors, for instance, is used consistently as a measure of how a network or brokerage is creating opportunities for the sales professionals associated with the organization. Stickiness (the amount of time a consumer stays on the site), and the number of page views, are other measurements used to demonstrate the commitment of the firm to create customer leads.

One other aspect of lead generation is currently seizing the attention of the industry—and it has just as much to do with good, old-fashioned legwork, as it does with advances in technology. This is the rise of the lead-centric model in residential real estate sales. This trend is becoming evident in all aspects of the industry, but in particular with the growth of real estate agent teams. While teams have been around for a long time, the Internet is enabling aggressive growth-oriented professionals to reach new levels of scale, and at the core of their success is the use of lead generation. Perhaps most interesting in this trend is that, unlike brokerage companies that recruit agents to bring new business, most teams recruit agents to work the leads that they generate for them. And these teams are proving adept at putting in place the systems needed to hold these agents accountable to the investments they are making in them and their leads. We believe the emergence of these teams is one of the more interesting things happening in the real estate industry today and we'll expand on this in the chapters to come.

◆ GAME PLAN:

- Stay informed about changes in policies that affect your business. MLS, Realtor® association; and, state-level and federal-level rules and regulations can impact the business environment in unexpected ways.

- The business of brokerage continues to be founded on the recruitment, development and retention of competent sales professionals. Leaders must continue to invest in value-added services that assist them with every aspect of their practices.

- Recognize that that there is no such thing as "one size fits all" for sales professionals. Their needs change over time due to their personal and business goals, aspirations, and sales styles.

- The last 30 years of brokerage have challenged firms by continually demanding more support for sales professionals—while the bidding war over them has driven down the share of brokerage-retained commission revenues. This trend will continue in the years ahead. Thus, cost management will be far more important going forward, and will require brokerage leaders to focus on the key metrics of their businesses.

- Brokerage firms will need to enhance their ability to either generate leads for their sales professionals or work in tandem with them to drive prospects their way.

Chapter 3

New Business Models and the Changing Economics of Brokerage

From market share, to transactions, to growth, there are many ways to measure success in residential brokerage. None is more important than profitability.

We saw in the previous chapter how waves of innovation disrupted the real estate industry since the 1970s. Some of those innovations— the profitable ones—withstood the test of time. The rest fell by the wayside.

Today, there are four basic business models for brokerages:

1. Traditional Graduated Commission Brokerages
2. High Commission Brokerages (such as RE/MAX)
3. Capped Commission Brokerages (such as Keller Williams)
4. Virtual Brokerages

Each has different characteristics and a different strategy for maximizing profitability.

The trends that affect the ability of brokerage firms to succeed in the future will be driven more by profit than by any other measurement. To succeed, brokers need to decide which model they want to pursue and set up the appropriate services and resources to support that strategy.

The focus of this chapter is understanding the forces that will shape the brokerage business. We'll discuss six key changes that have impacted the profitability picture over the last two decades, while taking a close look at how key metrics such as revenues, overhead, and profit margins are impacted by the different business models.

1. **Commission Revenues Rise and Fall**

2. **Commission Declines Prompt a Search for New Revenue Sources**

3. **Profit Margins Shrink**

4. **Brokerages Restructure**

5. **Customer Acquisition Costs are Assessed**

6. **New Business Models Impact Profits**

◆ Introduction

Despite time and numerous challenges, the revenue model for brokerage has remained remarkably consistent over time. The predictions that the residential brokerage industry would move to adopt more fee-for-service models—unbundled models where consumers select items from a checklist of services and pay for only what they want—never occurred in any meaningful way. The dominant form of compensation for residential real estate brokerage firms and sales professionals remains a commission based on the sales price of a home.

There are firms that charge flat fees for their services and certainly there are a few transactions where consumers and their sales professionals agree to some other form of payment for services. The totality of the market share of those using a real estate firm for service and who pay on a non-commission basis has not been measured with any great accuracy. Still, it is generally thought to be less than 5 percent of all transactions.

The practice of when and how the commission is paid has remained constant over the past 30 years. The seller of a home who lists the property with a sales professional agrees to pay a fixed percent of the settled gross price at closing to the listing brokerage firm. That listing brokerage firm pays the firm that procured the buyer a set percentage. This set percentage is most often agreed to ahead of time, and, in fact, is published for all other real estate professionals to see. The practice of paying both referral sources and co-op brokerage commissions is well-developed and understood.

The brokerage firms divide these revenues with each sales professional based on an agreed-upon compensation plan that is usually outlined in an agreement between the two parties. In some cases it could be said that what is truly happening is that sales professionals are sharing what they generate with their brokerage firm. In either case, while the percentage being paid to sales professionals has changed over time, as has the level of referral-fee charges and/or co-op percentages, the practice of how this occurs has remained constant.

◆ Commission Revenues Rise And Fall

While there's no standard commission rate in the country, most firms request and receive between 5 and 7 percent of the sales price from the seller when a home is closed. This percentage had drifted downward in the period from 1991 to 2005, when the housing market was strengthening and home prices were rising. It reversed course and began to climb through 2010 as the market weakened and home prices fell.

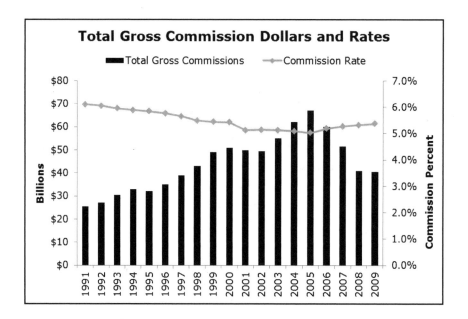

Even though the average commission rate fell between 1991 and 2005, the average price of the homes sold as well as the number of homes sold increased. Thus, total gross commission revenues grew substantially during those years.

Starting in 2005 and continuing through the end of 2010, total commission revenues reversed course and fell as both the number of homes being sold fell *and* the average price of homes being sold declined. These declines caused more dramatic decreases in industry-wide commission revenues despite the rise in the national average commission rate.

Over the last 20 years, some brokerage firms and sales professionals increased the total commission charges through the addition of a fixed-dollar commission charge over and above the fixed-percentage commission charged to the seller. Some charged this fee to property buyers in an attempt to make up for the loss of commission revenues in the face of declining commission rates during the 1991-2005 period. The charging of a commission fee to buyers was an entirely new practice. Before this, buyers had not been charged any specific fees by the brokerage firm for its services. There are no accurate measurements of how many brokerage firms or sales professionals are charging these additional flat-dollar fees to either sellers or buyers; but, it's believed to occur in only a minority of transactions.

Beginning primarily with the impact of the 100 percent commission programs in the mid-1980s, brokerage firms began to pay a higher share of the commission revenues to their sales professionals. As a result, net company revenues as a percent of gross revenues (variously described as Company Dollar, Company Revenue or Gross Margin) began to decline and have continued to decline over the last 25 years.

This shift was brought on by several dramatic changes. First was the ending of the non-solicitation clause of the NAR Code of Ethics, which freed both brokerage firms and sales professionals to more easily switch affiliations and/or recruit another brokerage firm's sales professionals. Secondly, it was generally recognized that the commission-sharing policies of the existing incumbent firms favored the lower-producing sales professionals. In other words, brokerage incomes from higher producers had been used to subsidize the firm's infrastructure costs, such as facilities, training, marketing and management.

However, the most important factor in shifting the percentage of commission revenues paid to sales professionals was the entry of the high-commission–concept program driven primarily by RE/MAX and, to a lesser extent, by Realty Executives. Under the traditional **Graduated Commission Model**, brokers share the gross commissions with their sales professionals; under the new **High Commission Model,** marketed by RE/MAX and Realty Executives, brokerage firms agreed to leave as much as 100 percent of the commission with their sales professionals, instead charging those professionals a fee for being part of their network. By the mid-1980s, these programs were in virtually every market in the United States and Canada. They inspired many higher-producing sales professionals to leave their existing firms and join firms affiliated with one of these two national organizations.

This trend accelerated for several years and prompted several leading traditional brokerage firms to enact their own 100-percent plans or to shift their existing graduated commission schedules to favor higher-percentage payments to their top sales professionals. Recognizing the contributions of sales professionals to generating business—as opposed to the contributions made by brokerage firms—continues to be a focus for many organizations today.

Two other business models that have accelerated this trend began to emerge in the early 1990s. One was the **Capped Company Revenue Model**, wherein the percentage shared between the brokerage firm and the sales professional was capped or limited to a set amount. While there are several firms offering this kind of program, it is most often associated with Keller Williams.

The other model that impacted the commission-sharing arrangements between brokerage firms and sales professionals is the **Virtual Brokerage Model**. At heart, these are high commission model firms that have dramatically reduced both the services they provide to professionals as well as the costs associated with being part of the company. These firms are essentially deep-discount models that have stripped away those brokerage costs considered secondary to some sales professionals' ability to conduct business. These 'non-essential' services often include personal office space, marketing and branding, and many other services that have typically been provided by brokerage firms.

Each of these brokerage models offers different levels of commission percentages or fee arrangements with sales professionals, resulting in entirely different revenue, cost and profit results. What brokerage firms found is that regardless of the business model, when operated carefully, each could be run profitably.

Model	Agent Fees	Agent Upside	Agent Services	Value Proposition	Target Agent	Companies
Graduated	Moderate	Moderate	High	Brand Model Flexibility	All	Century 21
High Commission	High	High	High	Upside Brand	Top Performers	Re/Max
Capped Company	Low	High	High	Upside Low Cost	All	Keller Williams
Virtual	Low	High	Low	Low Cost	Cost-Conscious	Solid Source

◆ Commission Declines Prompt A Search For New Revenue Sources

By the late 1980s, the leading traditional realty firms were not content to see their high-producing sales professionals walk out the door in search of higher commission payouts. Their reaction was to either offer their own 100-percent commission plans or to raise the commission share to their sales professionals—or both.

They began to recruit both new and existing sales professionals more aggressively than before. They also grew the size of their firms and their office spaces to accommodate these increases.

In addition, brokerage firms began to offer ancillary services such as mortgage, title insurance and other settlement services (core services) in an attempt to increase their service and revenue bases.

Another reaction to the decline in revenues retained by brokerage firms was the search for new sources of business that had the potential to carry higher margins. At that time, the main source of such business was relocation management. As mentioned in the previous chapter, throughout the 1980s and into the early 1990s, brokerage firms began to affiliate with national networks for the purpose of receiving relocation assignments. Some chose to affiliate with national networks that had a brand name (Coldwell Banker and Prudential) while others affiliated with independent networks that did not require a brand change, such as Homequity and Equitable.

Local and regional brokerage firms began to merge as the need to grow large-scale brokerage operations with large numbers of sales professionals was increasingly seen as the clearest path to profitability.

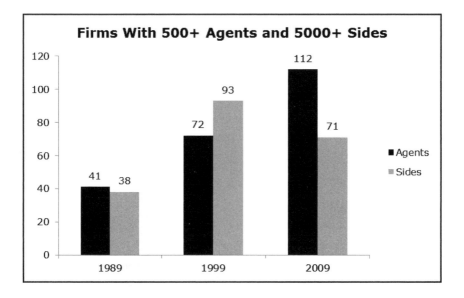

Firms With 500+ Agents and 5000+ Sides

Regardless of whether these firms affiliated with national brands or retained local brands, the number of firms having more than 500 sales professionals and doing more than 5,000 transactions a year exploded. Likewise, the number of firms engaged in core services grew rapidly throughout the 1990s.

In addition, while the number and volume of homes sold continued to increase, brokerage firms saw the percentage of revenues paid to sales professionals continue to increase, regardless of the business model. And while aggregate revenues were climbing (due to a robust housing sales market) brokerage costs were increasing as well.

By the late 1990s, a significant number of brokerage firms added additional flat commission charges on top of the commission percentage and began to levy such fees to buyers as well.

◆ Profit Margins Shrink

Despite the efforts of brokerage firms to offset the increased costs from both general business and the increased payments to their sales professionals, profit margins in brokerage firms declined in the years leading up to the market downturn in 2006. In the mid-1990s, a survey of brokerage firms—regardless of business model—showed that brokerage firms had pre-tax margins averaging 7 percent before tax. By 2005, these margins were nearing 4 percent on the same basis.

Revenues and profits from core services and additional commission charges played a large role in financing the increased requirements for technology and marketing throughout these years.

As a result of the downturn in housing sales, many brokerage firms, regardless of size, brand or model, now have small or even negative margins even including these additional service and revenue sources. As the market stabilizes and begins to recover, these firms must seek new ways to generate revenues and earnings and decrease fixed costs. They have no choice: The housing sales recovery is expected to be anemic in comparison with the 1985-2005 period. We'll have more to say on this in subsequent chapters.

◆ Brokerages Restructure

*Among the biggest challenges brokers face is staying relevant
in the conversation between the buyers and sellers of housing
and the real estate professional. Where can the broker
add the most value to that relationship,
and the one with their sales professionals?*

Alex Perriello, CEO
Realogy Franchise Group
Parsippany, New Jersey

The two largest costs of operating a brokerage firm are employment and occupancy. As you can see in the following chart on model profitability, each business model has different levels of costs expressed as a percentage of the firm's revenues. For traditional firms, employment and occupancy often represent well over 50 percent of all fixed costs. For lower-cost models, that number is much smaller.

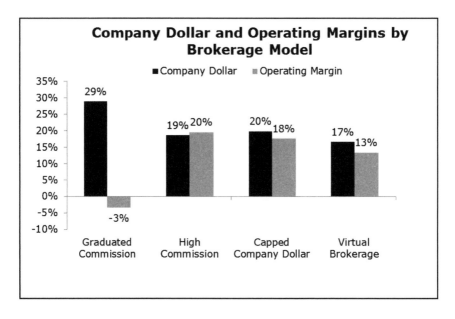

Fortunately for brokerage firms, more sales professionals have established home offices than ever before and, generally, are spending far less time at a company office. Obviously, the higher availability and lower cost of technology needed to operate a sales practice has had a significant influence on this trend. As a result, brokerage firms are reducing the fixed overhead of office space at a rapid pace.

At the same time, many leading brokerage firms are restructuring their management teams. Again, technology is playing a significant role in assisting brokerage firms to do so. Many firms have outsourced technology, marketing and education functions, reducing the need for staff to deliver services in these areas. This has enabled brokerage firms to deliver high-value service at a variable (not fixed) cost.

Training is one example. Nearly every firm now has the capability to deliver training and educational programs online directly to sales professionals without the need for a large meeting space. They can also deliver a wider array of educational opportunities. Most of the national networks offer their affiliated firms libraries of such materials, for example.

Brokerage firms have reduced their budgets for marketing and advertising, especially property-specific advertising. In the past, traditional brokerage firms might, for instance, have spent over half of their ad budgets on newspaper classifieds. The advent of the Internet and online listing portals has enabled brokerage firms to substantially reduce their spending in this area and to replace it with very low-cost online advertising. Most other advertising is directed at generating customers through various forms of Search Engine Optimization (SEO) and Search Engine Marketing (SEM), which are most often less expensive than the channels used in the past—plus, the results they generate can be measured far more precisely.

◆ Customer Acquisition Costs Are Assessed

If we allow those guys to have access to our listings (or our business), they'll capture our customers and sell them back to us.

Unattributed—but frequently voiced lament

This refrain, or one like it, is not attributed solely to online real estate aggregators. The theme was actually heard first in the 1970s as the relocation management industry began to charge referral fees to brokerage firms for corporate assignments. Originally, relocation management firms would buy a home from a transferring family and then sell it through a brokerage firm.

They would also refer that family to a brokerage firm in the destination location. There was no referral fee in those days. The corporate employer paid the fee for the service to a relocation management firm for assisting the family.

Beginning in the late 1970s, relocation management firms saw the revenue opportunity to be earned by placing these customer leads with brokerage firms. A referral fee would be paid by the brokerage to the relocation management firm. This has been the practice ever since.

Broker-to-broker referral networks actually predated the corporate relocation management firms by a dozen years or so. Homes for Living was formed in the 1950s. RELO was formed in 1960. ICR, Allpoints and Translo were formed in the 1960s and 1970s. The latter four networks today comprise one network called Leading Real Estate Companies of the World®. They were built to provide a framework wherein brokers could place referrals of families moving from one location to the next and receive a portion of the commission back as a referral fee.

At least initially, the referral fee charged by the broker-to-broker network was the same as that charged by the corporate relocation management firms. Over the years the percentage of the referral fee has generally risen for most players; there's much more variation today than in the past.

In this climate, arguments frequently break out between Internet lead management firms, online aggregators and others over the various charges for online marketing and/or referral fees. Some online marketers offer a brokerage firm or sales professionals the option of choosing how they want to pay for access to online customers. What's gaining recognition is that there's a cost to acquiring a customer. This includes in-house transactions between a brokerage firm's own sales professionals, co-ops with other brokerage firms' sales professionals, and leads from an online lead generator. There's also a cost for advertising and marketing—which, one supposes, causes phones to ring and prospective customers to reply to a contact made through an email inquiry.

The economics of brokerage firms are impacted by how they treat this 'cost of customer acquisition.' Most differentiate between business generated by their sales professionals, and leads or referrals generated by the brokerage firm's own efforts. Some 40 years ago, lead generation was a primary service that a brokerage provided to its sales professionals. As top sales professionals attained greater success in building their own businesses and their share of the commission revenue grew, and as brokerage firms grew larger in response, this core lead generation function fell relative to the other tools and resources that brokerage firms provided.

Most brokerage firms today recognize that the cost of customer acquisition is a part of every transaction. If you want to be in the business of providing business directly to your sales professionals, you'll have a cost that needs to be recaptured should you want to continue to provide that benefit.

◆ New Business Models Impact Profits

Given that a large proportion of sales professionals in the business do fewer than 5 transactions per year (35 percent of all sales professionals, NAR 2010 Member Study), we expect that the lowest-cost models may grow to have far larger shares of any given market in terms of the number of sales professionals they represent. Some of the lower-producing sales professionals are growing their businesses while others are shrinking theirs, yet the percentage of sales professionals in this category has remained relatively stable over the past 10 years. We expect it will remain so during the next 3-5 years as well.

The percentage of sales professionals who do make a full-time living in the residential brokerage business has also remained relatively flat. These would be sales professionals who complete >20 transactions per year (17 percent of all sales professionals). While sales professional teams have grown in recent years, the number of teams who have grown substantial levels of business (>50 transaction sides per year) has not increased dramatically in the past few years. However, we do expect both the number of high performance teams and the volume of business they produce to grow in the years ahead.

It's probable that some significant share of these sales professionals may gravitate over time to either the High Commission or Capped Company models as they have done historically. Some may even move to a lower-cost Virtual-Brokerage model, particularly those less in need of the support offered by the higher-cost, more full-service structures.

The remainder of sales professionals, who log between 6 and 20 transactions per year (41 percent of all sales professionals), will mix their selection between all four models as they do today. On the next page is a chart showing the relative differences in performance for each model for 2009.

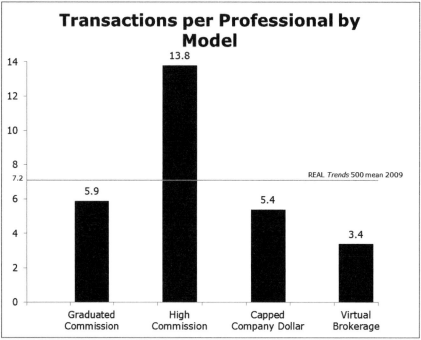

Source: REAL *Trends* 500 and Up-and-Comers, 2010

(Note: For the Keller Williams firms included in this study, the entirety of the net income was included before distribution to their profit-sharing program.)

The median for all sales professionals according to NAR for 2009 was 7.0. The mean for the REAL *Trends* 500 for 2009 was 7.2. Thus, three of the four models had average productivity for 2009 that was less than the industry average and only the High Commission Brokerage was higher—nearly twice the national average.

◆ Summary Of Models:

Here is a bit more detail on the different business models from a profit-and-loss perspective:

- Virtual Brokerage

These firms generally charge a flat monthly fee. They also typically charge a flat-dollar transaction fee. Some of the firms cap the number of transactions that sales professionals must pay on each year.

Some virtual brokerages also charge marketing and/or technology fees either as a flat-dollar amount per month or per transaction. Some also charge risk-management fees. These firms generally do not provide office space for sales professionals' personal use; instead, they field a few service center offices that allow for meeting space, supplies and reception.

- High Commission Brokerage

While this type of firm has been associated primarily with RE/MAX and Realty Executives affiliates, there are a growing number of firms that operate very similarly and are not affiliated with either. High commission brokerages generally pay out 100 percent of the gross commissions to the sales professionals, and charge them for office space and other services—often a combination of fixed and variable charges. Because these monthly fees are typically significant, High Commission firms tend to attract top performers who seek the high reward that this model offers and can afford the higher fees associated with being a member. This can also make it challenging for these firms to maintain membership when market conditions are challenging causing some agents to seek lower cost options.

- Capped Company Brokerage

This type of firm generally splits commissions with their sales professionals up to a predetermined amount, after which the sales professional keeps 100 percent of the commission dollar. Capped company firms sometimes charge additional fees for items that range from technology to risk-management fees. Keller Williams is the best known of the firms that follow this model and they have married this commission offering with a profit-sharing program that incents sales professionals to recruit others to the network. The combination of these value propositions has helped fuel their growth and is also leading to a growing number of firms looking to replicate their model.

- Graduated Commission Brokerage

Graduated commission brokerages are characterized by having a variety of commission-split programs, ranging from a graduated split program to some variations on the 100-percent commission programs. These firms tend to be larger in size. They usually charge for services such as technology and marketing in the form of fees, charge some form of additional flat-fee commission, and also frequently have substantial mortgage and settlement service operations.

Growth of business models 1990-2015 (est.)

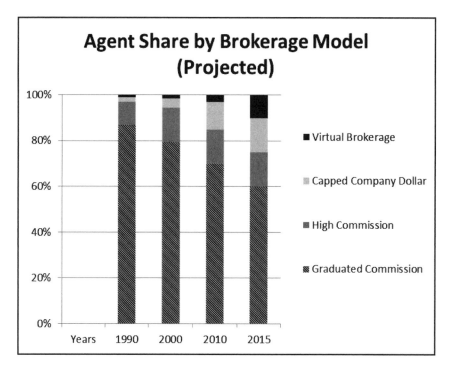

◆ High-Level Findings:

Which models offer firms the greatest potential for achieving solid profitability? We analyzed the data from the samples charted below to determine the correlations between costs—including occupancy, advertising, employment and other specific spending categories—and bottom-line profits:

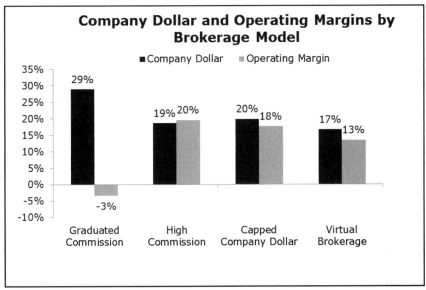

The chart above presents gross and net margin results from a sample of 10 of the best-performing brokerage firms from each model based on 2008 financial results.

- Occupancy costs are a significant factor in the ability of a residential brokerage firm to earn a profit.

The most profitable firms generally had the lowest occupancy costs. The three most profitable types of brokerages spent less than 14 percent of their Company Dollar on occupancy costs; two of the three most profitable had occupancy costs of less than 9 percent of Company Dollar. The Graduated Commission brokerages spent from 19 to 28 percent in the same category. Overall, traditional firms historically spend approximately 20 percent on occupancy.

- Advertising costs are not highly correlated with profitability.

Of the types of firms we measured, we found that high spending on marketing and advertising did not necessarily result in lower profitability. In fact, the highest profitability was experienced by the type of firm that spent the highest amount in this category. The Capped Company Dollar brokerage had the lowest advertising spending at about 3 percent of Company Dollar.

- Employment costs, which make up the largest category of expense regardless of the type of realty model used, are not highly correlated with profitability.

The most profitable model did not have the lowest employment costs, but rather was in the middle of the range of employment costs for all firms. Interestingly, the Virtual Brokerage spent the most in the category with an average of 57.3 percent of its Company Dollar on employment costs; the lowest was the Capped Company Dollar Brokerage with about 25.3 percent of total costs allocated to employment expenses.

- Lower general and administrative (G&A) costs correlate highly with profitability.

Generally, those firms with the lowest G&A have the highest profitability. In this category of spending, the lowest was the High Commission Brokerage with only 9.2 percent for G&A; the highest was the Capped Company Dollar Brokerage with 40.2 percent.

We also examined the impact of non-commission revenue sources on profitability and found that the move towards diversification has had a profound impact on a brokerage firm's ability to earn a profit. The Graduated Commission Brokerage had other revenues equal to 13 percent of Company Dollar while the Capped Company Dollar Brokerage had less than 4 percent on average.

Other revenues included profits from mortgage, title, escrow, property and casualty insurance, home warranty income, consumer fees, property management, commercial brokerage and relocation.

◆ GAME PLAN:

- One size does not fit all. Regardless of your commission and service plan, it will not appeal to all sales professionals—or even a majority of them. Measure your potential share to determine the right size for your firm.

- Your firm's core services need to be strengthened and broadened. The newest opportunity is for brokerage firms to offer property management and rental services as the percentage of homeowners, versus renters, declines. Increasingly, investors are seeking professional services for their rental properties creating new opportunities for brokerages to cultivate relationships with this important segment while building a new revenue source.

- Leads and prospects have grown in value. You should invest in your ability to generate prospects while also insuring that you are charging appropriately for the time and monies invested to generate company-driven business.

- You will have to decide whether the services your firm provides to consumers are worth a certain level of commission—and determine whether you will enforce a particular flat-fee level with your firm.

Chapter 4

Enter the Internet

The second of the **factors** disrupting the real estate industry is technology. The Internet has revolutionized the residential brokerage industry, inundating us with new tools and products that have changed the relationship with housing consumers forever. What has not happened is any major change to how consumers buy and sell homes – thus far.

In fact technology has been a two-edged sword. Although the consumer is empowered with access to information that was once controlled by the industry, we also have new tools that give us unprecedented access to and information about consumers. In addition, the move towards software-as-a-service or "cloud computing" will almost certainly lead to the consolidation of technology providers. Such consolidation should be positive for brokerage companies and their sales professionals as fewer firms provide more comprehensive and integrated platforms and higher customer ROI.

1. **What Happened to Brokerage?**

2. **They Must Love Us**

3. **Choices Made**

4. **Alternative History**

5. **At the Personal Level**

6. **Technology and Data Integration**

7. **New Internet-Based Business Models**

8. **The Role of the Sales Professional Has Changed Forever**

"The lions are coming - the lions are coming"

The specter of rampaging lions coming over the hill was, admittedly, the paranoid view of the Internet held by the brokerage industry in the early 1990s. We envisioned large well-capitalized, information-based companies, which would grab the MLS and housing information business and disintermediate brokers and sales professionals. Sales professionals would become low-paid vassals taking and processing orders. Housing consumers would abandon the commission-based service model and we would be working for hourly wages. And those wages would work out to far lower than what top sales professionals made in the past.

While not the exact words used by industry leadership, the message was clear. The Internet was a serious potential destroyer of the residential brokerage industry—its structure, practices and compensation. These fears were not without substance.

The Internet had already caused major disruptions in several seemingly well-established industries including music, books, photography and travel. Even newspapers appeared to be in jeopardy, deprived of one of their main sources of revenue—the income derived from classified advertising for jobs, autos, and of course, real estate. Fortunately, consumers seemed to have discovered that buying a home is a fundamentally different type of transaction than buying books, music, computers, airline tickets, or even shoes.

This is not surprising when you consider that there are four ways in which the housing transaction does not lend itself to e-commerce as well as many of these other noted examples:

1. **Size.** Generally speaking a home is the most expensive

transaction people engage in during their lives. Certainly the price tag dwarfs that of an airplane ticket, a book, or just about anything else.

2. **Complexity.** When consumers buy products online, they may look at the return policy or the different warranties. But that's about it in the way of terms and conditions. Again, there's no comparison with the complexity of a real estate transaction. The contract itself is intimidating; in addition, every line item is potentially subject to negotiation. Plus, there's the need to coordinate with mortgage brokers, banks or other lenders, inspectors, title insurance companies, and so on. Most consumers feel out of their depth—and rightly so.

3. **Frequency.** The best way to become familiar with the complexities described above is to do them on a regular basis. Consumers can get comfortable with online stock trading because they can afford to trade regularly. They get comfortable with the process and they figure it out. With the exception of a small percentage of investors, most people don't buy or sell homes very often. They understand that the legal and financial consequences of making a mistake far outweigh the amount they might save on commissions. Again, for anyone who doesn't have a lot of experience, it's a rational economic decision to work with experienced professionals.

4. **Uniqueness.** Finally there's a point that frequently gets overlooked. Houses aren't commodities. Each one is unique. You can't store them in a warehouse with a SKU bar code and ship them out when somebody orders one—like a book or even a pair of shoes. With housing, every piece of inventory is unique, even those in the same subdivision. As a result, consumers look to Realtors® to add value by knowing the points of distinction between different units or properties, and helping buyers evaluate the tradeoffs. People want to see their home, feel it and touch it. So far, no virtual visit can compare with the living, breathing experience of a home—a tremendous bulwark for Realtors® against the encroachments of the Internet.

As we have seen, the Internet did not turn out to be the ravaging pride of lions that many had feared. That said, its full effects have not yet been felt, and the warning message proved to be both timely and necessary for an industry that needed to figure out how to respond to yet another major disruption.

1. What Happened To Brokerage?

Let's start by reviewing the actual changes that technology has made in the way we do business. First, an estimated 90 percent of all homebuyers view homes online before they talk with a real estate professional. Second, nearly 40 percent of all buyers find the home they ultimately purchase online rather than through a real estate professional. And third, the percentage of housing consumers who find the sales professional they ultimately use online, has grown substantially in the past 10 years.

Yet the percent of housing consumers who use a real estate professional appears to be unchanged. Over 75 percent of all buyers and sellers still use a professional to assist them in buying or selling a home. And while consumers do enormous amounts of research about properties before they ever talk to a real estate professional, the process of purchasing and selling remains virtually the same as it was prior to the arrival of the Internet.

Yes, consumers are smarter about the market, more challenging of the professional's opinions, and more apt to question the conclusions that someone might offer. But they still use professionals to get the deal done.

◆ 2. They Must Love Us

How do customers feel about Realtors®? The old Merle Haggard song sums it up fairly accurately: "It's not love (but it's not bad)."
Surveys show that customer satisfaction with Realtors® remains

relatively unchanged, when comparing results from the pre- and post-Internet eras. Overall satisfaction remains about where it was 10 years ago.

That's good news right? Real estate professionals should take comfort from the fact that customer satisfaction hasn't dropped—even with the housing downturn and the fact that billions have been spent to provide content online and allow customers to shop without our input or control.

However, the fact that 90 percent of housing consumers go online to do their research rather than use a real estate professional definitely raises questions: Is it in fact easier for consumers to use the Internet to do research than relying on a professional? Or does it mean that consumers don't trust real estate professionals to deliver objective answers? It's easy to understand that a consumer might, on the spur-of-the-moment, see a house and then look up the information right away on a mobile device—rather than calling a sales professional. Similarly, casual future buyers or sellers might prefer to do some initial research without involving a sales professional; generally at this stage neither party wants to be bothered by the other.

Nevertheless, even small changes on the margin of a relationship can start to erode the professional's value proposition. As Marty Frame, president of Realtors® Property Resource notes,

The more we rely on the Internet to provide information to consumers, the closer the consumer gets to the actual transaction before they need a sales professional. There is some real danger that consumers may see that they know all they need to know and only need a sales professional to close a transaction – a far different value proposition than the traditional 'full' service relationship.

Today's sales professionals understand the importance of establishing a relationship over time. Usually the first agent interviewed is the one who gets to close the transaction. So we need to balance the comfort we derive from providing great information via the web with the need to keep the relationship active, so that we will indeed be the one who is called in when it is time to buy or sell. We need to actively manage the risk of customer independence by providing the right amount of value-added service in each individual relationship.

◆ 3. Choices Made

In her book, *March of Folly*, Barbara Tuchman told the story of nation states that made decisions they knew were inimical to their own self-interest. They knew of alternative strategies that were a better fit with their interests, yet they pursued the strategies that were destructive anyway. Some examples include the British Crown at the time of the Revolutionary War and America's war in Vietnam.

It's possible to view the real estate industry's response to the Internet through the same prism. Because the leadership felt that Microsoft, Yahoo! or others were going to invade and take over our industry information, a counterweight of similar design was needed. Hence, the Realtor Information Network and Realtor.com were born. These systems were designed to aggregate the information so that the consumer could find everything in one place, which happened to be under 'Realtor® control'. This was a one-size-fits-all solution.

Perhaps this was good for Realtors® at large. Perhaps it was a good strategy for the Realtor® association. It was certainly good for early investors in Realtor.com, who also had the foresight to cash-in their shares early. However, this early foray into technology led people to believe that if one national site was a good idea, then it would also make sense to develop multiple local/regional listing sites, hosted and managed by their respective Realtor® organizations and MLS systems. The added exposure would benefit members of the local Realtor® organization. So, now there were hundreds of sites hosted and managed for the benefit of all Realtors® (and at shared expense).

This also led to disputes with various Federal agencies about Realtor®

policies. Discussions about how data would and should be shared by and among brokerage firms, Realtor® and MLS associations led ultimately to the current policies for IDX sites and the use of Virtual Office Web sites (VOW).

Even so, brokerage firms and sales professionals persisted in thinking, "since being on one site is good being on multiple sites must be better." Thus, Trulia, Zillow, Yahoo! Real Estate and others were born. In turn, this led to firms like Point2, ListHub, and Postlets that assist brokerage firms and MLS with the distribution of listings to all of these sites. Then in 2010, Realtor.com purchased ListHub so that it, too, could assist brokerage firms with the distribution of listings to all of the sites—the very activity it was set up to prevent nearly 12 years earlier. It is also interesting to note that all three of these firms have recently been acquired by larger suitors, underlining the belief that listing distribution would be a strategic asset.

Duplication of effort was not restricted to the core listings database. Realtor.com, along with local MLS' and Associations, developed their own sets of tools for a multitude of processes for the benefit of all the members of the Realtor® association. In addition to websites and online tools, Realtor® associations added numerous technology tools, both desktop and online, for their memberships. While these efforts may have been good for the industry as a whole, they put the association in competition with its members in providing resources and tools that may have been a source of competitive advantage.

◆ 4. Alternative History

Other alternatives to this approach were available. One was the use of search software, similar to a Google search, that would have aggregated listings based on specified search criteria and displayed them in formats that were easily available, easy to construct and to install and use. Any firm wanting to participate could have acquired such software at very affordable terms so as to raise their own flag for their own properties. This platform also could have allowed each firm to do its own customization, its own online marketing and provide its own unique set of tools for both real estate professionals and housing consumers.

In essence, each firm would have been able to see each other's inventory while retaining the freedom to create its own online experience without regard to the rules imposed by the national and local Realtor®-owned-and-operated sites. There would have been significant competition to develop the most user-friendly site, the best 'search engine optimization' if you will, with a broader array of content (FSBO anyone?). The investment in such developments would have heightened competition and spurred even more creativity in both software and content to the consumer.

This solution looks more like advanced search as opposed to aggregated data sites. Instead, we have a system where there's little incentive for any brokerage firm, large or small, independent or nationally affiliated, to invest heavily in such developments. When any new tool or creative approach can be replicated by the national or local Realtor® site and when a brokerage firm must abide by the rules laid down by both NAR and their local Association, there's little incentive to invest in the kinds of developments seen in other businesses.

A similar outcome can be seen today in the travel industry. Online travel sites are now locked in a battle with various airlines as to how, when and where airline tickets can be purchased. The airlines want to customize their own experience so as to avoid further ruinous price wars. They want to offer a customized ticket buying experience and to have the customer deal directly with them—and not a third-party site— when booking travel. The airlines want their customers back, to have a direct relationship with them both through their own websites and with their own personnel.

So while MLS public sites and Realtor.com do serve a useful purpose, they also commoditize the experience consumers have online. To some extent, this reduces the competition by and between brokerage firms and national networks while also potentially ceding control of the consumer to national portals run by highly capitalized media and technology companies. This last point is particularly noteworthy, given that is exactly what Realtor® organizations set out to prevent in the first place.

◆ 5. At The Personal Level

The industry has glorified the role of the individual sales professional. Many firms and national networks strive to be the most professional-centric model, to build their models around the sales professional as the beginning and the end of the delivery of service to consumers.

That was a good strategy before the advent of cell phones, the Internet and mobile access. As many sales professionals are fond of saying, they only work part time – 18 hours a day, 7 days a week! When office hours were respected—when sales professionals could be reached at home only if absolutely necessary, when the office MLS terminal could only be accessed at the office—an individual could properly respond in a timely fashion with rare exceptions. Remember, this was back when many sales professionals hand-delivered offers to other sales professionals.

With the Internet and mobile access, many sales professionals feel overwhelmed by the amount of communication they are required to deal with every day. Emails and texts, Web requests, Internet leads, and phone calls all pour forth into the daily existence of the sales professional. There's little allowance for not returning emails or calls within a very short period of time, even when tied up with another customer. And, many sales professionals get emails from their sellers, from their website, from their buyers, from their office or company management, from their trainers and/or coaches, from their Association, from their MLS—not to mention friends and family. And all the while they're being told that the new standard for responsiveness is less than 10 minutes for a customer.

Now that this is the new reality of business, it's time to revisit the issue of whether a full-time individual sales professional can truly build their own business and still have a normal life.

The growth of *teams* is an outgrowth of the challenge for sales professionals to grow their businesses, maintain a high level of customer service for existing clients and have some personal time left over. The sheer volume of communications in today's world can overwhelm even the best-intentioned professionals— especially those working alone. And it can limit their ability to grow.

One last point about the impact of technology at the personal level— remember that the best real estate professionals are not necessarily technologists.

Sure, they've mastered certain tools (the use of the desktop, laptop and smartphone). But they haven't mastered all of the systems, software, applications and tools that the industry and its suppliers create each year. They can't keep up with the various websites where their listings are hosted or where valuable information can be found. There's simply too much of it for any one person to know inside and out.

As brokerage firms learn to outsource certain functions, so too have sales professionals begun to outsource their own marketing, educational and technological needs. The advance of Customer Relationship Management (CRM) and Transaction Management (TM) tools into the real estate brokerage marketplace are but two examples of new tools being designed in reaction to the overwhelming nature of the communication world that sales professionals face today.

◆ 6. Technology And Data Integration

Raw data is the least valuable type of business intelligence. Organize the data correctly and you have information, a step up in value. Apply experienced analysis to information and you get knowledge, the highest level in the information value chain.

To date, much of the technology developed for the residential real estate industry has had the effect of overloading professionals with data and information. This is due to a lack of integration. There are blocks of data controlled by differing parties with separate interests and with separate goals. First, there's the MLS; then the tax and property data; then there's the customer data; then the transaction data; the market data; the business operating data and the profit and loss results data. Let's not forget the advertising and marketing data, the online data and results. Data and information flood real estate professionals.

For example, let's take a look at a single source, the MLS listing data. There's no doubt that the MLS does a reasonable job integrating listing, sales and property data. But can it also correlate housing price changes with school scores or crime data? While a brokerage firm can now track the performance of its sales professionals (and everyone else's), can the firm correlate those results with the firm's or sales professional's investments in online marketing? While a profit-and-loss statement is a fairly straightforward exercise, can it be tied back to a profit-and-loss statement for each sales professional? These are just a few of the more pertinent questions for real estate professionals.

The solution is to have systems that can integrate multiple sources of information into a whole and deliver it in such a fashion that it becomes of highest and best use to the people who need it – thus knowledge.

To achieve this goal, brokerage firms need to recognize that software development should probably not be one of their core competencies. Instead of buying or building custom software, brokerages should be licensing cloud-based software that's built on technology and industry standards. Put another way, brokerage firms should be spending less time and money building and maintaining technology, and more working with qualified vendors who can deliver solutions that integrate across platforms and are updated automatically. This will help avoid the chronic problem we have seen of brokerage firms investing in proprietary systems that become either obsolete or costly to maintain. As more firms focus on articulating the solutions they need to build competitive advantage while outsourcing development and maintenance to others, we will see a flight to quality in real estate software applications that over time should be beneficial to the industry overall.

◆ 7. New Internet-Based Business Models

In addition to disrupting existing business models, the Internet has also spawned several entirely new forms of brokerage firms. There are firms that specialize in lead generation and aggregation, and firms built solely on the ability to convert online housing researchers into actual live homebuyers and sellers. These new firms have had, and will continue to have, an impact on the practice of brokerage.

Some of the better-known examples of online real estate firms are ZipRealty, Realestate.com and Redfin. Each employs online marketing tactics coupled with special attractive pricing for housing consumers. Their offers and incentives drive customer leads to sales professionals, in some cases their own and in other cases on a referral basis. Each of these firms has achieved some success in building market presence in several metropolitan markets. Although they have not achieved any dominant positions today, they are growing and cannot be ignored.

These firms employ some combination of SEO and SEM strategies as well as some more traditional marketing methods to attract customers. In many cases they offer commission rebates to heighten consumer interest in their offerings. They can afford to do so because they have little brick and mortar investment. At the same time, they attract sales professionals who place a high value on customer leads. These firms' business models assume that sales professionals who don't have to be involved as heavily in their own lead generation activities will have more time to dedicate to closing transactions. Thus they expect to achieve more sales on a per-person basis than is normal for the industry.

Another type of model that has grown since the advent of the Internet is one that combines expertise in SEO and SEM to drive leads directly to real estate professionals. Firms in this segment, like Market Leader, the Delta Media Group and many others, are neither brokerage companies nor media companies. Instead, they create marketing and advertising opportunities for brokerages and sales professionals often adding CRM and other tools to enhance the management of their businesses.

Each of these firms is the outgrowth of new technologies and business strategies that intelligently connect housing consumers who are searching online with the appropriate professional resources.

◆ 8. The Role Of The Sales Professional Has Changed Forever

In a relatively short time the value proposition of the sales professional has changed forever. Prior to the Internet, the sales professional was the gatekeeper of information about the housing market. Now the consumers can choose to procure that information on their own. Further, where the sales professional, and by extension the MLS, was the source of knowledge about the housing market, there are now a multitude of websites that can dispense such wisdom. Whether it's Realtor.com, Zillow, MLS or brokerage firm sites or other third-party sites, there exist today an abundance of sites that can provide access to information about the housing market.

Sales professionals have had to adjust to this new reality. Rather than being gatekeepers of information, Realtors® have gravitated toward being a gatekeeper of the transaction and the process. Along the way, many find themselves acting as a, kind of, adjunct advisor on the information that a consumer has located adding context and missing pieces. But the real focus is helping consumers navigate the complexities of the transaction and the process of getting to a closing.

Will technology ever replace sales professionals? For most consumers, given the complexity of the sale or purchase process and the infrequency that a consumer becomes a seller or buyer, we believe that will not be the case. That said, technology is impacting the way we interact with consumers, and that is certain to continue in the future.

◆ GAME PLAN:

- Brokerage firms and sales professionals should start to redesign their businesses around available and emerging technologies. Lead generation, CRM, and transaction management systems continue to evolve and are already beginning to have a dramatic and very positive impact on how some real estate professionals run their businesses.

- Brokerage firms still spend too much on print and institutional marketing relative to where their customers are searching for information on housing. Leading brokerages and sales professionals have transitioned their spend to vehicles they can more readily measure, and this flight to quality will accelerate in the years ahead.

- Response times to consumer inquiries must be improved to meet customer expectations and drive lead conversion rates.

- New models of engaging with consumers should be carefully evaluated by leading firms. While many of these models will be introduced by startups and new entrants, many of whom will fail, their ideas can often be adopted by more experienced industry players who can use them to enhance their own businesses.

Chapter 5

Changing Consumer Demographics

The last of the forces impacting our industry is the way in which the demographics of the housing consumer are changing.

The attempt to classify the people who buy, sell, and rent housing, along with their habits, practices, desires, and expectations, has grabbed enormous attention in the business world and popular culture. And an extraordinary amount of effort is being made to understand what features and benefits will best fit the new consumer segments that are developing.

In this chapter, we'll provide a look at the key consumer factors and behaviors that are impacting housing markets, concluding with the homebuyers and sellers of the future as well as how buyers will buy and how sellers will sell.

◆ Diminished Buying Power Of The Housing Consumer

The recent economic downturn has devastated consumers' net worth, career prospects, and income that is available to spend on housing. There's no end of statistics we could quote to make this point. But here are a few that do the job:

- For young people, job eliminations (7.8 million since 2007) and persistent unemployment (maintaining at over 9 percent at the end of 2010) make it very difficult for young adults to afford to move away from their parents' homes.

- Approximately 36 million of the 139 million employed workers in the United States suffered at least one spell of unemployment during the Great Recession.[1]

- Job losses were a key factor in mortgage delinquencies and foreclosures. For example, 7.1 percent of prime mortgages were seriously delinquent (90 days+) in the second quarter of 2010.[2] That compares with typical delinquency rates, even in the depth of previous recessions, of only about 2 percent[3].

- Median incomes for all households have dropped over the decade and will exit 2010 at lower levels than they entered it in 2000.

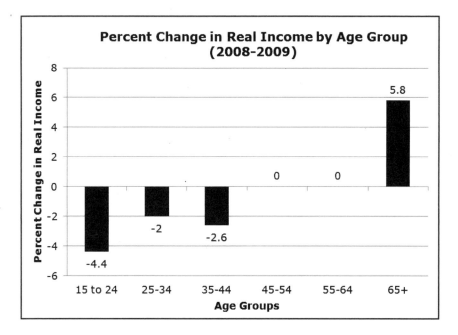

_____

1   Pew Research Center, September 2, 2010, "Most Re-Employed Workers Say They're Overqualified for Their New Job."
2   Source: HUD
3   Mortgage Bankers Association

When the housing bubble burst, home prices began declining at dizzying rates. There's no question that the reduction in home prices has made housing more affordable, as have historically low interest rates. Housing affordability is frequently measured as a percent of the gross income needed to cover mortgage debt as well as other debts, for a total debt load as a percentage of gross income.

Formerly, lending institutions limited the amount of total debt-to-gross-income ratios to about 30 percent. During the boom, it was frequently believed that a person buying a home could have a debt load over 50 percent. The thinking was that, as the house value increased, the debt ratio would correspondingly decline — and quickly bring the borrower back into a rational financial model.

Lenders of subprime mortgages and other exotic mortgage products such as NINJA Loans (No income, no jobs, and no assets) used this thinking to encourage people to buy more home than they could afford.

The deflation of housing values under the housing bust of the second half of the last decade has caused housing prices to be more affordable; however, lenders have returned to stricter standards, looking for larger down payments and lower debt loads.

The reduction in home prices has caused the debt ratios to drop from 32.7 percent of median household income at the height of the boom (2005), to just 18.9 percent in the first quarter of 2010. However, a more difficult lending environment, including higher down payment requirements of 20 percent, along with the debt ratio currently allowed (about 45 percent for all debt-related payments), makes loans much harder to obtain. These factors will place homeownership out of reach for many first-time buyers and minorities.[4]

---

4   The exception here is Asian minorities who have higher average
     real income than Caucasian.

◆ The Homebuyers Of The Future

The key trends in consumer behavior and how these will affect the housing market in the future are myriad and conflicting. We can't say for sure exactly how these trends will play out over time. Certainly, the impact of changing consumer demographics in the practice of buying and selling real estate is, and will be, enormous.

The three major government-produced trend reports (*American Community Survey*, *The Current Population Survey* and the *Housing Vacancy Survey*) each have different perspectives and projections on this question. What we do know is there are five key trends that will help determine who buys homes in the future, including reigning market forces, the increasing importance of immigrant and minority homebuyers, generational preferences, household composition, and the changes taking place in terms of who rents versus buys.

◆ Five Key Trends That Are Shaping Future Home Purchases And Sales:

1. Consumer and Market Forces Continue to Evolve and Interact

Household Formation

Household formation has slowed as young adults have been forced to delay creating their own households. In the longer term, as most young adults don't want to live with their parents, there will be pent-up demand for housing — both rental and purchased homes — once the job market recovers.

Marriage

Fewer people are getting married and fewer still are having children. Technically, this should increase total household formations, as two single-person households replace one married couple. However, the changes we see as a result may be in the *type* of preferred rental or owned home, including more multi-unit dwellings, smaller home sizes, homes nearer to transit, etc. In particular, this demographic shift raises the issue of whether the larger homes that were built during the real estate boom will, in general, prove to be attractive to couples or partners without children.

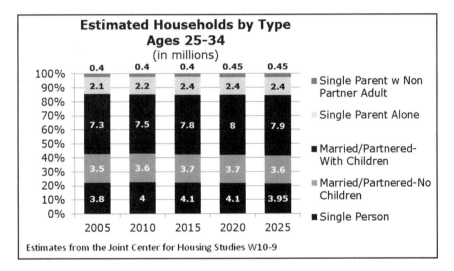

Joblessness and Immigration

Joblessness suppresses household formation, particularly among the young adults who are just entering the workforce. It also suppresses immigration — so there's less competition for the jobs that exist. However, lower immigration means lower overall household formation and lower housing sales.

With each generation, the contribution of immigrants to the total population increases. The children of these immigrants have incomes more like existing native-born populations than their foreign-born parents, so they're an important source of home sales when they become adults.

Lower Home Prices

Lower home prices, driven by the dramatic fall-off in housing sales, combined with government programs to support home sales, allow first-time buyers to enter the market for single family homes. This was less of an option for them in the middle of the last decade; however, unemployment rates and stricter lending standards are counterbalancing this positive, as these tend to suppress the rate of home purchases.

Lower home prices, while benefiting first-time homebuyers, have caused many people to be significantly underwater in their homes. This means they can't move, thus suppressing repeat purchases, move-up buying, and retirement and second-home purchases.

Subprime Mortgage Inventory

While most of the subprime mortgage inventory is gone, our nation's job losses have also impacted the prime conventional mortgage market and the rural home market. The total mortgage delinquency and foreclosure numbers in this market will lag the rest of the market because prime borrowers typically receive unemployment insurance and have other resources such as 401(k)s on which to draw before defaulting on loans.

Rural loans may also lag as the government figures out how to stave off foreclosures in rural areas. Finally, we'll see the continuing failure of loans that have been renegotiated.

Mobility

Overall, from 2005 to 2008, mobility (people able to move to take new jobs) declined 12.6 percent. It then stabilized in 2009. It should be noted here that the need to live close to a new job while waiting out the market revival should increase the need for rental properties.

2. Immigrants And Minorities Are Playing An Increasing
Role In Home Buying

There's a growing debate about the status of illegal immigrants in the
United States. The economic rationale for greater diligence in both
preventing entry and removing those already here is that they cost
more than they return to the Treasury in taxes and take jobs from legal
U.S. residents.

From a housing market standpoint however, minorities and
immigrants are an increasingly important source of both household
formation and buying and owning homes.

Of the projected 11.8 million household growth from 2010 to 2020,
less than one third (29 percent) are Caucasians, while 71 percent are
minorities.[5]

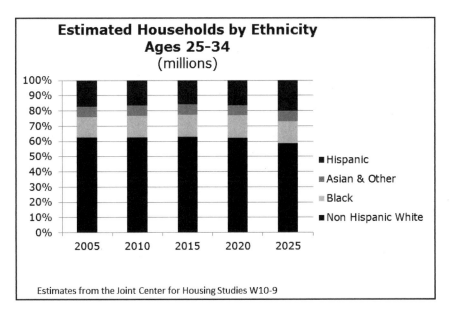

5   George S. Masnick, Daniel McCue, and Eric S. Belsky, JCHS.
     "Updated 2010-2025 Household and new Home Demand Projections,"
     September 2010, W10-9© Page 20

Together, minorities and immigrants represent more than half of first-time homebuyers (54%), and one-third (32%) of repeat buyers. [6]

At the peak of the bubble, there were approximately 7.8 million illegal immigrants in the United States. With job losses, particularly in construction (-1.3 million jobs), this number fell by about 1 million as immigrants returned to their native countries, according to The Office of Immigration Statistics at the Department of Homeland Security[7.]

If and when we see an increase in immigration—with a concurrent increase in potential households and therefore homeownership (some portion)—it will largely be driven by the return of full employment to the economy, and greater political support of immigration in general.

3. Gen Xers And Boomers Are Mostly Repeat Buyers

Most housing statisticians and prognosticators point to Gen Xers and Boomers as remaining in the homeowner camp in the coming years. Of those that do move, most will sell their existing home and purchase another to replace it.

Gen X is in the primary family formation ages and ready for a move-up purchase. This generation was significantly smaller than either the Boomers or Millennials, at around 67 million of the U.S. population. They are comprised of children of the older (leading edge) of the Boomers. This is a generation that is typically marrying later, buying less house than they can actually afford, and having fewer children.

Baby Boomers are a very large age group (born 1946-1964 = 80 million people) that has mostly established their households. The Boomers are a generation that started with gusto, having been encouraged by their parents, born in the depression, to try different things. Boomers, as a group, have watched their nest egg investments decline significantly

---

6   JCHS, IBID Page 4
7   JCHS, IBID page 12

in value—in both stocks and bonds and home equity, just as they were getting ready to retire.[8]

We'll talk further about the buying preferences of these age groups later in the chapter.

4. Buying Will Be More Favorable Than Renting

The drop in home prices and in mortgage rates (and thus, mortgage payments as well) is approaching equivalency with the gross rental cost, making it possible for more people to make the buy-versus-rent decision in favor of buying. In 2006, the average home price was $204,156, the mortgage rate 6.4 percent and the after-tax mortgage payment $1,079. This was significantly higher than the gross rents average of $778 for that year. In 2009, the average home price was $172,100, the average mortgage rate 5 percent and the after-tax mortgage payment $835, while gross rents averaged $825.

At the same time, the lower average real income and joblessness experienced by Americans, particularly younger adults, makes even these seemingly modest payments versus 2006 unaffordable. As the difference between the cost of owning a home on a monthly basis (mortgage alone) and gross rents drops to zero, there will be an increased desire for ownership.

Most likely the next big real estate buyer group is the Millennials (the generation comprised of later children of Boomers). They are projected to be less likely to be married or have children in the household.

As you can see from the chart below, those who buy will have most likely lived with parents or rented previously. This is completely consistent with the larger portion of the total buyer population being first-time rather than repeat buyers.

---

8   Pew Center Research: "Boomers are Most Glum Generation"

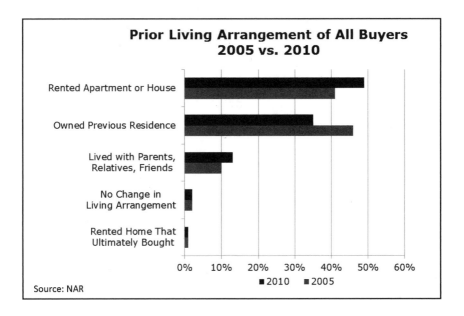

While the desire to own a home will remain the primary reason they buy, *when* they purchase may be strongly driven by tax credits or other incentives. The newer generation of first-time buyers generally has more issues with making commitments. Obviously, buying a home and maintaining it is a huge commitment, so they'll probably need a reason to do it earlier versus later.

5. What Consumers Are Buying Is Changing

While most buyers continue to prefer the detached single-family home (75%), first-time buyers have actually increased their preference for detached single-family homes. Other research suggests that although these homes may be their preference, the difference from the past is that the preferred homes be in densely-developed, suburban neighborhoods, near public transportation and entertainment.

The Concord Group, a consultancy to some of the nation's leading developers and financial institutions, recently did an extensive survey focused on *20-to-34-year-old professionals* who had earned a college degree and had a job (less representative of the total age group, but more consistent with those who might have the wherewithal to buy).

It provides a glimpse of what new buyers will be looking for when they purchase real estate.

Even though the majority held a positive attitude toward the economic recovery, the survey respondents primarily saw themselves renting for now and buying a residence within a three-to-five-year time frame.

However, because this is a young and thus presumably more mobile group, if they do buy, factors like their ability to resell and pay off a mortgage early will be very important.

This group of buyers sees their next residence as a condominium or apartment versus a house with a yard, for example. It's interesting to note that 28 percent of this group expects to buy a single-family home with a yard; this is approximately the same percentage that is projected to marry and have children sometime between 20 and 34 years of age.

This group also has very different ideas about what they value in a residence, and again, it has very little to do with the traditional suburban experience. They're looking for close proximity to grocery stores, restaurants, work, parks and bars. The things they least value are proximity to schools, playgrounds, auto repairs, places of worship and childcare (see the chart below). Another important value is being close to alternative means of transportation. So while they may not want to live in an urban loft, they want to be closer to the action.

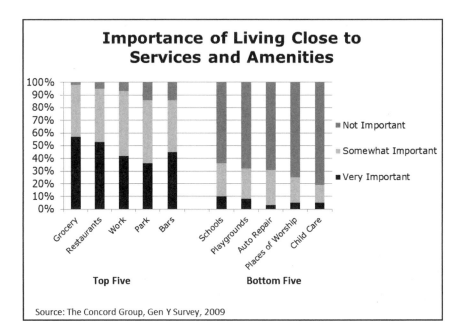

Source: The Concord Group, Gen Y Survey, 2009

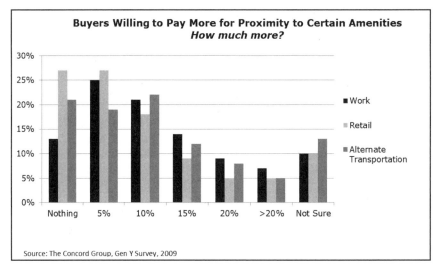

Source: The Concord Group, Gen Y Survey, 2009

◆ How Do Buyers Buy Homes?

Almost all buyers first look online for properties that are for sale, according to the most recent study by the National Association of Realtors®. The one exception is the 65+ age crowd, who still tend to contact a real estate professional first.

• Millennials And Gen X Consumers

First-time buyers who sit on the cusp of Millennials and Gen X consumers (30 years of age) are more likely than older buyers to talk with friends or relatives about the home-buying process, but even for this group, the professional is a very important resource. Some 92 percent of all first-time homebuyers used the Internet as an information source, and 88 percent of first-time buyers used a professional for information, according to NAR 2010 Profiles of Home Buyer and Home Sellers. The usefulness of the professional has actually increased on an overall basis since 2005, as has the Internet.

However, this did not translate into the professional being the source of the homes these buyers ended up purchasing. From 2001 to 2010, the percentage of buyers who found their homes through the professional dropped. Those who found homes through the Internet rose from 8 percent in 2001 to 37 percent in 2010.

When REAL *Trends* last did a survey (*The Consumer Tsunami,* August 2006) of the behavior of homebuyers, yard signs were an important third source of information, because buyers drove around to find homes and neighborhoods. But this has dwindled from 15 percent of buyers finding their home by this method, to 11 percent in 2010. This may be due to the fact that the Internet is becoming much better at providing detailed pictures of neighborhoods (e.g., Google Earth), homes for sale, etc.

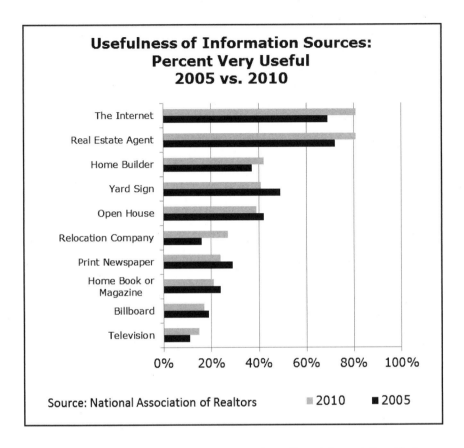

Usefulness of Information Sources: Percent Very Useful 2005 vs. 2010

Source: National Association of Realtors   ▪ 2010   ▪ 2005

For first-time buyers, and these are mostly Millennials and Gen X, the process may be overwhelming, and *finding the right property was what they considered the most difficult part of the process*, followed by saving for the down payment and getting a mortgage.

First-time buyers are taking a long time to search for properties. For all buyers, the average weeks searched has risen to 16 weeks in 2009, from 12 in 2002. Both first-time buyers and repeat buyers searched for an average of two weeks prior to contacting a professional.

In spite of the downturn in net worth, many parents will still be helping with the down payment and, unlike Gen X, Millennials trust their parents' advice.

- Boomers

Boomers (ages 46 to 65) are beginning to retire. This huge generation (80+ million people) was expected to rewrite the way people retire. They were going to move to warm places and live in active adult communities. Unfortunately, many of them don't have the money they need to retire. According to the Center for Economic Policy Research in Washington, D.C., the combination of the drop in the stock market and the bursting of the housing bubble cost the Boomer generation horrendously. People aged 45 to 54 today lost an average of 45 percent of their net worth from 2004 to 2009. That represents a drop from $172,400 in 2004 to just $94,200 in 2009 (all amounts in 2009 dollars). [9]

For those aged 55 to 64, the Center for Economic Policy Research suggests that the losses were even worse.

As a result of this catastrophic loss, most homeowners aged 45 to 64 have little or no equity in their homes. This, of course, makes it very difficult for people to sell their home to move or buy another home, or to move to the active adult communities they may have considered for retirement.

Boomers want single-story plans to avoid trouble with tired knees; they want low maintenance and the ability to live near their kids. Employment, which traditionally would be winding down for the older portion of this 20-year cohort—people aged 54 to 65—will continue to be important. Due to the crash of their net worth, many Boomers are working longer.

Sixty percent of Boomers have said that they will need to delay retirement.[10] In the McKinsey Study, 85 percent of respondents said they would continue to work after retirement.[11] So Boomers will be competing with the Millennials for jobs as employment recovers, versus retiring and letting the younger generation start their independent lives.

---

9   David Rosnick and Dean Baker, Center for Economic and Policy Research, "The Wealth of the Baby Boom Cohorts After the Collapse of the Housing Bubble."
10   Pew Research Center, "Baby Boomers Approach 65 – Glumly"
11   Cited in Builder Magazine, July 7, 2009, IBID

What is particularly worrisome about this, and has been shown repeatedly, is that how and when the younger generation starts their career has a great deal to do with where they end up in the class hierarchy. If they have more menial, low-wage jobs in the first years of their career; it will negatively affect their total life earnings dramatically.

For Boomers, however, many want to simply stay where they are now. An AARP study, whose findings dovetail with those of the American Housing Survey and Census, found that about 80 percent of this age group want to stay in their existing home as long as possible.

NAR suggests that 11 percent of homebuyers over 50 years of age did make a purchase in some type of senior-focused housing. About half of these purchases were single-family detached homes (51%) in suburban areas (46%). However, 31 percent were in condos or townhomes, 32 percent were in small town/rural areas and 20 percent were located in an urban or central city environment.

◆ Who Are The Sellers And How Will They Sell?

Of course, one of the biggest questions of all is: Who will sell their home—and who will lose it? There are currently, according to NAR, 3.7 million homes on the market. This is a vastly different number than that cited by CoreLogic, which says 4.7 million are on the market. Right now, there are already 2.1 million additional homes that are in the early stages of foreclosure.

NAR suggests that in the home-selling situation among repeat buyers, 12 percent of those who had not yet sold their home were either renting to others or the house was currently vacant. Looking at the numbers, this percentage has to exclude those houses that have been foreclosed and are vacant, or which may have been rented to others. According to the Census Bureau, there are currently 19 million vacant homes, as of first-quarter 2010.

The median age of sellers from 2010 was 49 years old, up from 46 years old in 2009.

Most home sellers are using professionals (88%), while only 9 percent of homes are being sold by owner (FSBO: For Sale by Owner). When we look at the level of service people who used a professional received, the picture becomes clearer. Some 11 percent of the people used a professional only to place the home in the MLS. This hardly counts as using a professional.

An additional 8 percent used a limited set of services requested by the seller. So, if we add the portion where the professional only placed the house in the MLS, we have a combined FSBO/Other of about 22 percent, a very different picture.

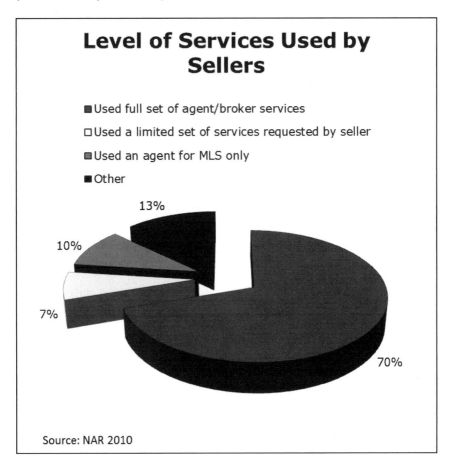

Level of Services Used by Sellers

■ Used full set of agent/broker services

□ Used a limited set of services requested by seller

■ Used an agent for MLS only

■ Other

13%

10%

7%

70%

Source: NAR 2010

Pricing the home appropriately seems the most critically important aspect of the home sale process.

What sellers have indicated they want most from real estate professionals, is to help them price their home competitively (23%), followed by finding a buyer (21%), and helping the seller market the home to potential buyers. For circumstances where the real estate professional listed the home on the MLS and performed fewer if any other additional services, the importance of pricing rose to 26 percent. Sellers who got the price right got at or close to 100 percent of their asking price and sold quickly. In REAL *Trends'* 2005 work on how sellers chose among various models to sell their house, having the home priced appropriately was the most important experience for the seller (77%).

Source: NAR

Sellers clearly want more contemporary marketing tools. Of particular note are videos and social networking sites. Sellers know that social networking sites allow a younger generation of potential buyers to see the house without going to an open house, to ask their friends for comments on the potential house; and, to share thoughts and ideas about the process and potential homes, with their friends and parents.

Even for very busy Gen X and Boomer buyers, videos and other media that allow them to see more of the neighborhoods and potential houses before actually touring the homes in person have proven very time-efficient. They also serve as an effective productivity tool for the professionals, allowing people to be more selective with the homes they ask the professional to show them. The younger generation wants to see more homes before they buy, and the absolute compensation for professionals has been reduced due to reduced home prices.

The chart below ranks the marketing tools and other media used by potential buyers in researching, and making decisions about, home purchases:

	Used	Very Useful
Listing on the Internet	91%	81%
Yard Sign	79%	49%
Open House	56%	42%
Print Newspaper Ad	28%	29%
Real Estate Magazine	25%	24%
Other Websites with listings	25%	
Direct Mail	16%	
Video	12%	
Social Networking Sites	5%	
Television	2%	11%
Video Hosting Websites	2%	
Other	5%	

◆ GAME PLAN:

- The demographics of who is buying homes is rapidly changing. It's critical to stay in touch with who the buyers will be in the areas where you conduct business. For example, immigrants and minorities will be buying homes in increasing numbers. In those regions of the U.S. where they will tend to move for job opportunities or cultural affinities, this will have far greater implications.

- Household compositions are changing, as are the kinds of homes buyers are looking for, and the attributes offered by desired neighborhoods. Builders and real estate professionals must continue to educate themselves and act on the home characteristics sought by the newer generations of buyers.

- The proportion of first-time buyers is growing. These buyers are careful and demanding. Expect to show more homes and be able to answer more questions about future resale values and housing market projections.

- The Internet's impact on home buying and selling continues to grow. Creative uses of the Internet and other new media are powerful marketing tools for the newer generations of buyers and sellers. From Twitter to YouTube, utilizing these tools effectively to attract customers will give you an edge.

- Pricing homes competitively is still the number-one most important service that sellers expect from real estate professionals. As a result, this is an area where tools and training for professionals can be particularly important.

Chapter 6

Ten Trends that will Drive the Next Five Years

In talking about the disruptive forces of competition, technology, and demographics, it's essential to note that, for the most part, our industry has done an excellent job of absorbing rapid change. Of course, the bull market for housing had a lot to do with that. When housing prices double and concurrently volume increases substantially, the rapidly increasing pie enables those who execute effectively to tolerate quite a bit of adversity.

To quantify this, just look at the long-term average annual amount of sales commissions, which had held steady at around $40 billion per year. At the height of the bull market, this number climbed to nearly $80 billion per year. Then came the great recession, and downturn in housing, which brought commissions back down, below the levels of ten years earlier.

Very few industries can survive that kind of cratering without an extremely high level of attrition. In real estate, while many professionals washed out, many others streamed in after being laid off from jobs in other industries. As a result, while the pie got cut in half, the number of people trying to make a living in real estate stayed near record levels.

And that's where we find ourselves today. We've largely adjusted to disruptive new business models which have now become a part of our reality. We're still dealing with the Internet and incorporating new ways of doing business into our models. At the same time, we are dealing with significant changes in the housing consumer and their needs. And of course we are doing all of this in the backdrop of a slow housing market where we all must work much harder to earn the same commissions.

It's an environment that demands all of our attention and responsiveness. To succeed we need to have a keen understanding of how our environment will continue to evolve and what it will take to win in the years ahead. That's why we've identified the ten trends that we believe that real estate industry professionals will need to watch carefully. No matter which strategy or business model you pursue, understanding these ten trends and what they will mean for your business will put you ahead of the game.

◆ The Ten Trends That Will Drive The Next Five Years:

1. **A Slow Recovery in Housing Sales and Prices**

2. **Changing Consumer Demographics**

3. **Pressure on Commission Levels**

4. **The Continued Advance of New Business Models and Industry Segmentation**

5. **The Growing Importance of Lead Generation**

6. **The Use of Integrated Technology Platforms**

7. **The Evolution of How Consumers will Select Real Estate Professionals**

8. **The Importance of Leadership**

9. **The Emergence of Real Estate Teams**

10. **A Stiffening Regulatory Environment**

1. A Slow Recovery In Housing Sales And Prices

Currently, the overhang in inventory combined with the lower than expected growth of households is delaying the time when the housing market will return to health. Shadow inventory is another major factor in restraining prices. This refers to the historically high percentage of homes whose owners are delinquent on their mortgage payments. The houses are not yet in foreclosure, but have the potential to come onto the market, and at a discounted price.

Despite all of these factors, over the next three to five years housing sales are expected to recover from their lows of the third and fourth quarter of 2010. Annualized existing home sales are projected to be 5.1 to 5.2 million in 2011 with the potential for a small surprise on the upside of that level. New home sales are projected to come in around 400,000 to 450,000 for 2011, again with some potential for some upside improvement.

For 2012 through 2015, projections from NAR, Fannie Mae and others indicate that sales will show steady growth (by historical standards) towards 5.7 to 5.9 million existing home sales and 650,000 to 750,000 new home sales at the end of the next five years.

These projections are based on a steady lowering of unemployment, the continuation of low mortgage interest rates and a return to normal levels of consumer confidence. Many believe that due to fiscal challenges at the state and federal level, unemployment will remain higher than normal for the next few years and that interest rates will climb as state and federal governments continue to borrow record amounts to fund deficits. Both of these scenarios would generally cause the economy to grow more slowly than normal after a recession and limit the growth in housing sales.

The growth of the economy will have a great impact on household formation and immigration. Both of these key factors fell during the recession and, should growth be slower than expected, housing sales, particularly to first-time homebuyers, will be sluggish. The other factor that will impact housing sales is the 71 percent of new households that are expected to be minorities—the very groups who have seen shrinking homeownership rates over the past 3-4 years and are the most impacted by the foreclosure crisis. The ability for these families to purchase housing given tightened lending standards and lack of income growth may reduce their homeownership rates in the short term even further.

Prices of homes for 2011 are projected to be soft in many markets across the country due to the continued overhang of inventory. Current inventories are estimated between 3.8 and 4.5 million homes with an additional 1.5 to 2.5 million distressed homes in some stage of delinquency or foreclosure. At this time estimates of the potential of this shadow inventory vary greatly. Nonetheless, for 2011 and 2012 there's likely to be an overhang of inventory that will keep a lid on prices in most markets and in most price ranges.

Given the small increases in unit sales and neutral-to-small increases in home prices expected for the next two to three years, the industry will show small and steady increases, but no return to robust growth is likely in the near to medium term. There will be markets where inventories come back into balance more quickly, and where employment and incomes rise faster resulting in larger gains than are the norm nationally.

In this type of market, leaders will want to be extremely cautious and thoughtful about how they invest in their business. In an environment where the pie is not growing significantly, you have to look critically at strategies to grow market share. Historically, the solution has been to recruit more real estate professionals. Today, it's uncertain how effective that strategy is going to be. Because real estate professionals have the economic power, the margin brokers can make on each incremental Realtor® is not very good.

As a result, success in this market will require a coherent and focused strategy, and the conscientious deployment of resources on the professionals and consumers you wish to attract, and the competitive advantages you will need to win their business.

2. Changing Consumer Demographics

Generational and cultural segments will matter more in the future than they have in the past. There are now four generations of home buyers and sellers in the market: The Traditionals (>66 years of age), the Boomers (47-65 years), the Generation X (35-47 years) and the Millennials (<34). This represents the first time in the modern age where there are four distinct generational groups engaged in the purchase and sale of homes. As Pat Riley, president of Allen Tate Companies notes,

We have a unique situation where we are now serving four distinct generations, each with their own housing needs and requirements and each selling or purchasing in different ways. One of our great challenges will be to ensure that we have a diverse group of sales professionals who mirror these demographics.

That's because there is little crossover of generations during the agent selection process. When housing consumers choose a real estate professional they tend to choose someone of approximately the same age. For instance, rarely do Boomer sales professionals serve Gen X or Millennial housing consumers.

The same is true of ethnicity. That's important because minorities, many of them immigrants, are expected to make up 71 percent of all new households over the next ten years.

Real estate professionals need to keep a watchful eye on the buying preferences of these demographic groups and broker/owners need to be sure that they are building a team of professionals who are most apt to reach their target consumers. Why develop a sales force with expertise in suburban subdivisions, if you're in a market where most people want a condo where they can live, work, play and shop—all in the same neighborhood?

Here's a brief overview of generational characteristics, with the caveat that, like any generalization, these are subject to a great variety of individual exceptions.

Millennials will make up the majority of the first-time home buyers in the next five years. They tend to marry later, with the possible exception of the minority or immigrant sub-segments of this group. Rather than suburban single-family detached residences, a large share of this generation will want lofts, townhomes, apartments and other low maintenance styles of housing. They will make the shift to larger housing once they begin to have families and, at least among some minority and immigrant populations, the average size of the family is larger than Non-Hispanic Caucasian households.

Generation X (Gen X) is a mixed group. The older members of this generation have likely already purchased their first home and many have traded up as they have started their families. Generally, they prefer more suburban neighborhoods as they seek schools and other amenities that support the family. Gen X homeowners were hit hard by the downturn in housing due to the timing of when they purchased their first homes and where prices were during this period. Thus, their ability to "move-up" may be negatively impacted for several years.

Baby Boomers—at least the older ones—are beginning to plan for retirement. This group accounts for a large share of the purchase of second homes and retirement residences. Their children (mainly the aforementioned Millennials and Gen Xers) have grown and moved away, thus leaving Boomers with the need for more efficient living quarters. This generation has also been hit hard by the downturn in housing and may delay the move to smaller quarters due to little-to-negative equity in their current homes.

Traditionals are in their retirement years and, like the oldest of the Boomers, are moving into smaller and more efficient living quarters. The oldest of the Traditionals are also seeking maintenance-free living arrangements and a growing segment is seeking assisted living quarters. This generation remains important purchasers of second homes as well.

The Millennials and Gen Xers will account for the majority of home purchases over the next 3-5 years. On a volume basis, the Boomers will likely still account for the largest percentage due to their current holdings and the size the generation itself.

Currently, the average real estate sales person is older and of different ethnicity than the majority of homebuyers that are expected to enter the market in the next five years. Brokers should think carefully about recruiting more young people, and people who are most connected to the consumers that they wish to serve. Similarly, agents who come from different countries, speak different languages, and/or represent growing minority groups may prove to offer a significant competitive advantage to forward thinking brokerages in many communities.

3. Pressure On Commission Levels

The average national residential commission rate fell in a virtual straight line from 1991 to 2005, falling from 6.1 percent to 5.02 percent. With the downturn in the market the average rate increased back to 5.36 percent as of the end of 2009. 2010 should show a similar result.

Numerous studies show that it was competition among sales professionals for relatively scarce listings that was the main culprit for falling commissions—not the Internet. The average commission rate fell more prior to the entry of the Internet and public listing portals than it did afterwards. And the rate increased after 2005 even with further developments and greater use of the Internet by housing consumers.

Sales professionals reported in various focus groups that they were willing to grant discounts on their charges in order to win business during the period of robust growth. This is not surprising, given that housing prices (and therefore total commissions) grew at a substantial rate, more than making up for reductions in the commission rate itself.

Over the next 3-5 years the market will return to balance and the competition for listings will once again be fierce. Additionally, we will see growth in the number of brokerage firms using newer business models (100 percent commission, capped company dollar and virtual brokerages) that have lower incentives to drive a commission standard with their firms. These factors will both lead to downward pressure on the commission rate.

In the past, most of the downward pressure has been felt on the listing side of the transaction. Today, pressure on the buy side of transactions is beginning to build and will continue to do so for two reasons. First, there are firms, such as ZipRealty, Redfin and others, whose offers of service include a commission rebate on the purchase side. Second, an emerging practice among buyers is to deal directly with listing professionals, removing a buy side professional from the transaction. These homebuyers request a rebate of some portion of the commission that would normally be allocated to the buyer's sales professional.

In order to make up for declining commission levels, brokers and sales professionals will need to manage their costs and be creative in seeking out steady sources of transaction volume. We have already seen this trend at work during this downturn as many professionals have built competencies in working foreclosures or short sales that they would never have considered spending time on before the market turned.

4. The Continued Advance Of New Business Models And Industry Segmentation

For the past thirty years, each succeeding business model has generally raised the commission percentage payable to the sales professional and lowered the commission percentage retained by the brokerage. To put it another way, sales professionals, over time, have sought, and will continue to seek, the most profitable environments in which to operate their personal businesses. For example, big producers can afford the high desk fees charged by 100% commission shops, because they expect to recoup the outlay in short order by maintaining the commissions they earn. The majority of Realtors® however don't have frequent or large enough sales to take on those higher desk fees. Instead, many have moved to Capped Commission brokers where the overhead is lower, and in the future, more of these agents will consider Virtual Brokerages where they are lower still.

Traditional brokerages have evolved and built flexible models to retain their sales professionals. While this worked well for many in the past, the downside is by trying to be everything to everyone, the brokerage can easily find itself in a situation where its value proposition is no longer the most attractive to any of the sales professionals that it hopes to target. Industry economics will pressure brokerage firms to select the business model that is right for them and to focus their energies and limited resources on the professionals that will fit that model.

Let's look at this idea in a bit more detail. When sales volumes were soaring and the ability of lower cost models to offer competitive support programs was limited or of little interest to most sales professionals, most brokerage firms and sales professionals didn't have to choose one model over another. They adapted on a case-by-case basis to meet new competition while carrying the legacy costs of their existing business model.

Given the expectation that sales volumes will not recover to the double digit growth rates of the 1985-2005 period, the new lower-cost models are causing everyone in the industry to reexamine the tug-of-war between what services brokerages can deliver and what sales professionals value in turn from their brokerage firm.

It's not just brokers who must determine what value proposition they are offering to sales professionals—who they see and treat like customers. Sales professionals also need to sort through the various brokerage offerings carefully to find the one that best fits their needs.

Will these choices always be rational and based on an absolute "dollars-and-cents" basis? Of course not, any more than consumers of all kinds purchase their goods and services outside real estate. Sales professionals will make their choice of brokerage based on business potential, commission and fee programs, quality of the firm and its reputation, friends they may have within a firm, and the support package offered by the firm.

In the future, this will put enormous pressure on brokerage firms to build brokerage business models that offer the right packages of support services at prices and terms that allow them to reasonably grow, and make a return from the business.

It means that a firm can't be a full-service brokerage, and have the lowest cost offer for sales professionals. It also means that brokerage firms can't be the lowest-cost provider, and offer the fullest range of services for sales professionals.

In short, brokerage firms can't be all things to all sales professionals, and thrive.

5.   The Growing Importance Of Lead Generation

While our industry's professional-centric focus will continue over the next five years, a new focus of great importance is also emerging and will play a big role in our future. That focus is on leads, and the tools needed to close them.

While leads have always been important, the growth of technology has accelerated their role as a currency in today's real estate industry. Currently, virtually every national network is engaged in some lead generation activities. Search Engine Optimization (SEO), Search Engine Marketing (SEM), the integration of IDX sites, and the use of advanced data mining and database marketing are just a few examples of early investments made by agents, brokerage firms, and franchises to build their competency in this important area. As such, leads are emerging as a new currency for the industry.

Of course, as we have all learned, the lead is not even half the battle. The majority of sales professionals (and in fact most small business people) have little training in the cultivation of leads. As a result, contact management, lead cultivation, and customer relationship management systems can and will play a huge role in determining which agents and companies are most successful. After all, lead generation is a numbers game, and only easy-to-use lead cultivation systems will enable professionals to build and manage the thousands of relationships they will need to manage in order to become a top performer. All of which brings us to our next trend.

6. The Use Of Integrated Technology Platforms

The real estate industry has long suffered from the lack of integrated systems for handling both the property data and consumer data pertaining to a real estate transaction and the applications to make them work seamlessly.

For too long there's been a mindset of thinking, "Technology is critical to our future. Therefore, we're going to build a proprietary system that will be a competitive advantage for us." This approach has not been a good use of precious industry capital as brokerages around the country find themselves trying to maintain and integrate legacy systems, at great cost, both in terms of money and time-to-market.

At the same time, recent announcements from leading franchise networks demonstrate that the ante will continue to be raised in terms of technology, and what professionals will expect from their firm or franchise. As expectations continue to increase, most of the innovative, but small and under-capitalized technology firms which play a big role in our space, will be unable to keep up, especially as brokerage firms come to expect more in terms of critical issues like the security of customer data, privacy, and business continuity.

As a result, we expect that, over time, more business will migrate to cloud-based offerings from larger providers that can integrate effectively with other offerings, thereby relieving brokerages of the burden of building and maintaining costly proprietary systems. These firms – those that choose to invest in integrated systems that can be updated rapidly – will likely build a cost advantage while reducing the time it takes them to bring to market new innovative features.

7. The Evolution Of How Consumers Will Select Real Estate Professionals

Consumers are already using online sources of information in addition to traditional ones when they think about choosing a Realtor®. Of course social media has to be front-and-center in this discussion. This is true simply because many conversations that once happened in person or over the phone are now taking place online.

We could easily restate this trend as follows: "Referrals from friends and family will continue to be important." What's new is that those referrals are happening on Facebook, Twitter, Yelp, and other websites. Leading Realtors® have already learned this, and this trend will certainly continue.

Consumers are also locating and choosing sales professionals and brokerage firms based on information they find on real estate portals created by consumer housing related firms such as banks, membership organizations, and even retail firms.

For example, both USAA and Bank of America have set up, or are in the process of setting up, fully functional real estate portals. Customers who use the main websites of these two firms can visit the real estate section to search listings and research sales professionals' experience and qualifications.

In addition to these new channels, there are a variety of efforts to place some form of sales professional rankings online. Firms such as Trulia and Zillow are both experimenting with these new consumer-facing tools. Some Realtor® associations are also doing the same. There are also sites such as Angie's List and Yelp, which have more generic service ratings and a growing number of reviews of real estate sales professionals as well. All of these sites are eager to offer these services both to meet perceived consumer demand as well as to increase their prominence with search engines which often promote just this type of content in their results.

So while the majority of housing consumers are likely to continue to reach out to friends and associates to locate and select a sales professional, the way in which they do this will continue to transition online, and specifically to social media sites. As a result, growth oriented agents, and particularly those focused on serving Millennials and Gen Xers, will need to be sure to build their reputations and their networks online.

8. The Importance Of Leadership

What factors have the greatest effect on the performance of brokerage firms over long periods of time? Research shows that it is not size, location, brand or business model. While these factors are important, the one that matters most is the capability, intelligence and work ethic of the leader of a brokerage firm.

It's not that hard to understand why. These are tumultuous times. Business leaders have had to deal with three disruptive factors that are subjecting the industry to constant change. That's where leaders prove their worth. Leadership is about making tough choices, and we know that in the next five years, the all-things-to-all-people strategy is simply not going to work.

Leaders will need to decide what business strategy they want to follow, and define a Game Plan to reach their strategic goals. This involves telling your staff and sales professionals what your brand stands for and who you are culturally, even when those decisions involve short term pain.

The day-to-day responsibilities of brokers and sales managers will vary depending on the business model of a brokerage firm. For full-service brokerage firms, sales managers must be good at recruiting, coaching, mentoring, supervising, reviewing transactions, and putting deals together. They must also be familiar with how to work with in-house loan officers and settlement service providers. For some high commission concept and capped company commission firms, the roles are not quite as extensive.

Unfortunately, few brokerage firms, regardless of business model or size, are investing any appreciable amounts into the development of future leadership for sales or company management. Today the average age of the leadership team at all levels, for most brokerage firms, is well above 60 years. Clearly it's time to start developing new talent with the background, skills, and temperament needed to make tough decisions and hold people, including themselves, accountable.

9. The Emergence Of Real Estate Teams

We've already talked extensively about the massive shift in our industry from a broker-centric to a professional-centric model. You might say that the next logical step has been a refinement of that model: How sales professionals can effectively take the professional-centric model to the next level. In other words, how they 'get big' and ramp up their income by delegating specialized tasks to other team members. We are seeing more and more of this as top professionals invest in lead generation, and then build out their teams to work those leads.

Interestingly, these teams offer a compelling value proposition to other sales professionals as well. Many sales professionals are all too eager to forgo the costs of investing in their own marketing, prospecting, and brand building activities, when they can make a good living working with more customers on a high performing team.

The keys to this model are process, specialization, and accountability as team leaders define specific tasks for each team member, and hold agents and staff accountable to the successful execution of these tasks.

With the advance of lead generation and CRM systems, there are no known limits on real estate teams. The largest teams drive as much volume as brokerage firms ranked on the REAL *Trends* 500 report. There are hundreds of teams in North America, some with two people and a few with over 20. Their total numbers are growing at this time and we expect they will continue to do so. The economics are compelling regardless of the brokerage firm or geography, and we expect that many agents and brokerage firms alike can learn a great deal from the strategies being pursued by these business leaders.

10. A Stiffening Regulatory Environment

There's no question that, since the housing crash, there's been a rush to point fingers at the causes. In this climate, our legislators and rule-makers have been busy creating new regulations that purport to 'prevent' an economic disruption of this magnitude in the future.

We're not going to weigh in on the effectiveness of much of this new sausage-making, but many new laws and regulations are on the books at all levels of government, and there's much more to come.

Along with more regulation, because of the straitened circumstances experienced by governments at all levels, we see great potential for higher taxation of homeownership. This includes changes in homeownership supports, such as, a potential elimination or reduction in the mortgage interest deduction, as well as, the prospect of rising property taxes.

Additionally, areas such as RESPA, Truth in Lending, energy audits and other legal requirements will receive far more scrutiny than in the past.

You think residential real estate transactions are already abundantly complex? There's more to come. Along with heightened scrutiny from federal and state regulatory bodies in the area of appraisals, lending, fair housing and inspections, there's a high likelihood of new home energy–related audits, higher transfer fees and taxes, and more scrutiny from housing consumers.

One large issue is the fate of GSEs like Fannie Mae and Freddie Mac. As of this writing, the future of these mortgage giants is uncertain. What appears certain is that they won't be in a position to provide the kind of ready-made secondary market for residential real estate loans they had in the past. This may mean higher-priced residential mortgages with far more stringent requirements for borrowers.

The Dodd-Frank Wall Street Reform and Consumer Protection Act passed in 2010 also have several provisions that may tighten lending further. One other area that will impact residential real estate sales professionals (and brokerage firms) will be increased privacy regulations that impact how, when and where information may be or must be shared, stored and protected. Already some national banks are rearranging their relationships with residential brokerage firms under joint ventures and marketing alliances due to the new regulatory requirements. Most of these changes will not be favorable to residential brokerage firms.

There are no indications at this time that there will be heightened regulation of real estate sales professionals—except for increased continuing education requirements.

Stay tuned, and be sure to make your voice heard by our elected officials both privately and through our industry's associations.

Chapter 7

Game Plan: How Brokerage Firms can Thrive in the Future

Game Plan is a pragmatic look at the real estate industry: why it is what it is today, and what it will take to succeed over the next five years. Based on our review of the ten trends, we know that major challenges confront us. Now it's time to get to work and lay out some concrete suggestions that will enable you to build your business, focus your resources, and maximize your prospects for success.

◆ The Five Steps To Thriving As A Brokerage Firm:

1. **Set Your Objectives**

2. **Build a Leadership Team**

3. **Select a Business Model**

4. **Define Your Market**

5. **Establish a Strong Culture**

1. Set Your Objectives

Don't underestimate the importance of objective setting as you prepare your business for success over the next five years. "*Sure,*" you're thinking, "*everybody knows you have to start at the beginning...*"

If the idea of objective setting seems too basic, then you may want to remind yourself that our industry has just gone through its worst downturn since the great depression. You may have survived, but you certainly have colleagues—and competent ones at that—who didn't. With that in mind, you might want to ask yourself, again, what you want and can realistically expect to get out of the real estate business over the next five years.

Is it about being the biggest? The best? The most profitable?

If those questions are too generic, get more specific. Ask yourself what profit margin you'd like to target. What unique assets, resources, or skills do you possess? What opportunities or niches do you see that you can capitalize on and build competitive advantage around?

Or do you have more personal reasons? You may want to create your own work environment, with the power to select the people who are part of the organization. Or you may see real estate as a way of building community.

Whatever your personal motivation is, develop your vision in detail. Write down what you want to establish in terms of the culture, the size of the firm, financial objectives and what your role will be in the organization.

Build a business plan that identifies the resources, tools and personnel you need to achieve your vision. Be sure to include the tactics and steps you will take and means you have of measuring success. Develop a written business plan against which you can measure your results and progress towards your objectives. And always remember, objectives should be clearly measurable; because in the end, what gets measured gets managed.

2. Build A Leadership Team

After you've written out your objectives, the next step in the Game Plan is to start thinking about your leadership team. We know that the most important factors determining the success of any brokerage firm are the capabilities of the leader of the organization, and the skills and dedication of the overall leadership team.

But that doesn't necessarily mean you should immediately hire the biggest producers or people that you've known before and liked. To survive—and thrive—over the next five years, you need to be selective and choose individuals that have the skill sets and temperaments that will work best for the organization and are committed to your objectives.

You need to ask yourself, "What do we stand for? Is this going to be a transparent organization? Is decision making going to be top down or consensus-driven? Will the structure be hierarchical or flat? Some of these decisions will be impacted by the business model you choose, and that's the subject of the next section. Just bear in mind that sometimes the same questions have to be looked at several times in different contexts: What is the role of the agent? What consumers will we target, and with what type and level of services? Based on the answers to these and other similar questions, you then need to decide the roles you need, and the type of people you will hire to fill those roles.

Of course, while hiring is important, even more important is to identify techniques you will use to build future leaders within your firm. It takes a considerable investment of time and resources to train leaders, so you need to have a plan for how to equip them with the knowledge and experience they will need to be most effective.

Invest your own time in developing these future leaders and consider bringing in other leaders from within and outside the industry to supplement your training program. The use of outside business leaders is an effective way to broaden the knowledge base of your future leadership team and bring valuable business lessons over from other markets.

As usual, it's essential to develop a means of measuring the progress of your future leaders against the requirements of your organization. Maintain a regular schedule of discussions with your future leaders to determine a) how well they are absorbing the lessons, b) how well they work with other members of the team and c) how well they are performing against the expectations you have set out for them.

3. Select A Business Model

Throughout *Game Plan*, we've been talking about the four primary business models of brokerage today: the traditional graduated commission plan, the high commission plan, the capped commission plan, and the virtual brokerage plan.

Each of the four models has proven that, if managed well, they can be highly profitable and have reasonable growth prospects. But the time is ending when a firm can be a little of many different models. Success in the years ahead will require focus, and focus will require more specialization of models than has been practiced by most traditional firms in the past.

Understand that which model sales professionals favor will change over time and is not always based solely on the economics of the offering. But the trend has been, and will likely continue to be, for more sales professionals to seek models that provide lower costs.

In this section we'll walk through some of the differences between the models from an owner's perspective. You'll see how the models tend to impact the P&L, what resources you'll be expected to provide, with special emphasis on what kind of technology you'll need.

Let's start with the good news: Rumors of the demise of our industry have been greatly exaggerated. All of the data shows that the rate of utilization of real estate professionals has held steady, despite the widespread availability of technology and information that was previously reserved for professionals. The plain truth is that consumers are going to continue to buy and sell homes, and the vast majority will do so with the assistance of a real estate professional.

The bad news is that there will continue to be pressure on commissions. Consumers will continue to seek concessions from Realtors, who, in turn, will seek to hang their licenses with firms that provide the most favorable trade-off between risk and reward. We look at that subject from the sales professionals' perspective in the next chapter. Here we focus on the same equation from the perspective of the broker/owner.

Suffice it to say, the choice of model makes a huge difference on the P&L. In the traditional brokerage industry the margins are already thin, and most of the forces and trends we have discussed in this book will only increase the pressure on our margins.

Part of the challenge is, no-doubt, the professional-centric model, and how much of the value delivery we have effectively outsourced to agents. Many brokerages have evolved to be service providers and landlords, while agents are expected to build, cultivate, and service their book of business largely on their own. In those cases, is it any wonder that owners are keeping less and less of the total commission pie?

Contrast this with the model being pursued by some of the top performing teams we discussed earlier. When you look closely at the best of these teams, what you find is a hierarchical and process-driven business with clear accountability for all those involved. In the case of these teams, it is the team, not the agent, that is responsible for providing and funding core functions such as advertising, lead generation, lead cultivation, and technology.

Instead of recruiting agents to bring *their* customers, these teams are recruiting agents to work the leads that the team is generating. That adds real cost to the model, but it's also very clear what value that team is bringing, and that value is captured in how commission splits are structured for all involved.

Don't get us wrong. We know we are describing only a tiny fraction of all teams, and that teaming is no nirvana. We point it out here because we see this more accountable, more lead-centric model as offering brokerage firms a new and profitable line of business that they can add to their existing P&L by creating e-teams focused on working company-generated business. This model is, of course, complimentary to the existing business while offering a profitable new revenue stream to the brokerage just like relocation departments, and later, core services did in decades past. Innovative brokerages are doing this today, and it's a trend that we expect will grow, and one you should consider. While execution varies by model, we have seen it work effectively in graduated, high commission, and capped models.

4. Define Your Market

Game Plan is about understanding change, adapting to it and, hopefully, thriving from it. We've talked about how dramatically the demographics of the housing consumer are changing. While this is true, in some geographic areas more than others, it is an important factor in all markets. This represents a significant opportunity for brokers who can establish themselves in segments of the market where the growth is going to be.

Of course there are many different ways to segment the real estate market. You can look at demographics, geography, types of communities, price points, transaction types, and many other segments and niches.

Now, as the leader of a sizable brokerage company, expertise in one of these niches will probably not be enough to build your business around. However, building a competency in identifying and targeting different segments of the market may very well be a powerful strategy, even for sizable firms. Many in the professional-centric model have historically left segmenting and targeting to the agents themselves. This is fine, but the less value the brokerage brings to the agent who is successful in building their business, the smaller their share of the commissions from that agent over time.

In contrast, a firm, that is willing to invest to build specialties in targeting these niches and in developing their people to target them, will have far more leverage on a long term basis. This is especially true if the firm is willing to invest in the marketing, technology, and training resources that will help agents succeed in pursuing these areas, while also building the firm's brand with the consumers targeted.

To make this strategy more tangible, let's look at just one potential example. Today there are 1.1 million Realtors® in the U.S., and their average age is 54 years old. Incredibly this is up from 51, just 3 years ago. More incredibly, there are 245,000 less Realtors® today than 3 years ago, and 220,000 of those losses have come from Realtors® aged 49 and under.

As we discussed earlier, Millennials and Gen Xers will make up a significant percentage of our customers in the years ahead, and most customers tend to select Realtors® who are similar to them. This points to a big opportunity for any brokerage that is focused on serving these younger buyers to build a competency in working with these groups and an agent sales force that is most likely to succeed with them.

Of course, the same strategy can be applied to the ethnic groups that may be prominent in your area, to targeting other niches from the second home or luxury segment, or to short sales. Regardless of the target, the key is focus.

5. Establish A Strong Culture

The development of ties that create a bond between the leadership team and sales professionals is highly important.

Whereas in the past this was mostly tied to the 'office' culture, in the future these bonds will be more closely aligned with the personal and business interests of each individual within an organization.

For real estate companies to offer the highest value they have to provide a "center" that sales professionals see value in. Build a sense of community, online and off line, to build the most enduring organization.

Pam O'Connor, CEO
Leading Real Estate Companies of the World

This is especially true as sales professionals spend less time in an office and more time working from home or in a 'mobile' environment.

Building a strong culture starts with several component parts. They are:

- Vision

- Transparency

- Communication

- Accountability

- Empowerment

- Discipline

- Community

Vision

For leaders in realty services, vision can be defined as the ability to articulate what the organization wants to achieve and the beliefs and principles that support that objective. Without a clear idea of achievable goals and the behaviors that are acceptable to reach them, the organization is more a collective of individuals than a focused entity. Where the organization wants to go, and what they believe about themselves, is the essence of vision.

Leaders are active and persistent in being involved in spreading their vision throughout their organization. Vision is not a business plan or a strategy. It's not a mission statement. In a real sense, it's the sum of what a leader believes should matter most to those who work for the firm as well as the experience its customers have.

People within an organization need to have a clear sense of what matters to the leadership and what it wants to achieve. With such clarity, great results can happen. Without it, consistent results are far less likely.

Transparency

A transparent organization is one that is free from pretense or deceit, is readily understood, and is characterized by visibility or accessibility of information. Firms need to share many kinds of information, as well as be very open and accessible. In addition, opinions and input are sought frequently from those in the firm. Staff and sales professionals from leading organizations feel that they're participants, not mere observers, in the organization's plans.

Transparency encourages respect and trust in leading organizations. It gives those in the organization a higher sense of comfort knowing their leaders are out in the industry and picking up information on trends.

There is a direct relationship between an organization's level of transparency, its level of trust, and its level of success.

Communication

To thrive in the future, the leadership of any organization in a competitive market must create an environment where information moves freely throughout the firm. Vertical communication, where information moves from leadership to the organization, and vice versa, is equally as important as horizontal communication among peers, and across lines of authority.

Firms that will thrive will focus on ensuring that information is shared frequently with staff and sales professionals. In addition, staff and sales professionals should have ample opportunity to exchange information with each other.

Leaders would do well to focus on bottom up communication and on horizontal communication across operating units and lines of authority. Horizontal communication is related to being a transparent organization. It's also viewed as idea exchange. The exchange of information and the question-and-answer session remain at the heart of those firms that will thrive.

Accountability

*I'm not going to lie awake at night worrying
about people who are not lying awake at night."*

Larry Kendall, co-founder,
Ninja Selling and The Group Inc.

Accountability is defined as an obligation or willingness to accept responsibility or to account for one's actions and results. In the business world, results are often measured by gains and losses in sales, profits, stock price and market share.

Financial results are only one main outcome of business activity. In the residential realty business, firms measure results in numerous ways. The yardstick could be profits, market share, sales totals or capture rates of mortgage or title insurance. The numerous designations and awards for achievement in sales or revenues also can measure results.

To thrive in the future, leaders will have to build accountability for results in areas that have not received much attention in the past. Along with profit and loss, and balance sheet issues, leaders must keep track of new metrics. Some of the more important are:

* Productivity of sales professionals
* Revenues and costs of sales professionals
* Returns from online marketing including traffic, lead generation, lead conversion, and more
* Market share of the firm, its offices, and its sales professionals within the types of segments and niches we discussed earlier

Patrick Lencioni's book, *The Five Temptations of a CEO*, lists, as one temptation, the CEO's inability to be clear about expected results and the accountability relating to these results. Many CEOs also want to be liked instead of holding their senior team accountable for results. This is endemic in the residential realty business.

For many, but not all firms, accountability for behavior will also matter greatly. It's well known that many sales professionals will not engage in the activities and practices (such as returning phone calls or emails) that it takes to build a successful career. Similarly there are countless monies and hours invested in training and guiding sales managers to recruit new sales professionals. Yet in both cases sales professionals and sales managers are retained even when their behaviors and work practices show that they're not performing as planned. This lack of accountability impacts the company's bottom line in many different ways.

Empowerment

Empowerment is the act of establishing a system or environment that allows people to have more control and responsibility over their actions. Some organizations can establish and support an environment where people can act without asking permission. As a result, they find that their people are more creative and more involved in attaining successful outcomes than firms that don't.

Empowering people in your organization sets the stage for creativity and innovation. Decisions affecting everyday commerce should be handled at the lowest possible levels in the organization.

Moving everyday decisions to a lower level may not seem to add to an organization's creativity, but it tends to free up senior leaders' time for researching and creating new growth strategies and making other key decisions.

Discipline

Discipline is defined as orderly or prescribed conduct or pattern of behavior; a rule or system of rules governing conduct or activity. Many people would say that realty service firms are best when they're entrepreneurial, making decisions by instinct and valuing individual skills over the organization. That may have been true in the past and is likely still the case for some of the industry today.

However, firms that wish to thrive in the future can no longer afford the luxury of making decisions by gut instinct alone. That era is drawing to a close. What will continue to rise in importance will be data-driven decision-making and far more discipline about when, where and at what level investments of the firm's resources will take place.

As Lencioni discusses in *The Five Temptations of a CEO*, failing to clarify what you expect of your people is one of a leader's deadliest sins. Without systems and the discipline to follow them, firms will either be drowned by too much or too little information, or have decisions made without workable plans for implementation.

Community

As the use of technology multiplies and realty firms reduce their office space as a result, building a sense of community among the sales professionals and staff of a realty enterprise will take on more importance. With the passing of an office-based community, whether through downsizing or due to the business model, sales professionals will be more mobile and less likely to appear in an organized office environment to conduct their business. It's also an outcome of the necessary cost reductions in the residential brokerage business in the future.

Where offices had developed their own cultures, habits and practices, sales professionals will be far less likely to gather on a regular formal or informal basis. In this environment, firms desiring to thrive should focus proactively on building culture and community based on common interests both personal and professional. For personal interests, it could be anything from sports to art, dining or reading. In business, it could be idea-sharing in social media, the effective use of marketing tools, or new ways to prospect.

Being involved in the community must be a high priority. Whether it's to help your sales professionals connect better (and become experts in) their respective communities, there's no stronger way to build a sense of community than to involve the people of a firm in giving back to the communities where they do business. This not only connects your people to the community, it satisfies a deep desire among sales professionals to be associated with an organization that does so on a regular basis.

Chapter 8

Game Plan: How Sales Professionals can Thrive in the Future

Game Plan:

The residential real estate world is complex and challenging. We've talked about this at length in previous chapters. Yet despite a very tough and competitive climate, many sales professionals succeed— and flourish. Those who are happy with the outcomes they're achieving are typically more focused and disciplined than the rest. Just as important, they set objectives for their business, they understand the market they are going after, *and* they understand the risks and investments that they are undertaking.

In other words, successful sales professionals tend to be those that have a strategy; one that is a fit with who they are; and, one they are focused on carrying out.

◆ The Five Steps To Thriving As A Sales Professional

1. **Set Your Personal Objectives**

2. **Become an Expert in Your Market or Niche**

3. **Develop Systems for Prospecting in Your Market or Niche**

4. **Build Systems for Servicing Leads and Customers**

5. **Build Your Brand**

1. Set Your Personal Objectives

Whether you're completely new to real estate, or have hundreds of sales under your belt, we believe the answers to the following questions should be the foundation of your business:

What do you want to achieve in residential real estate sales?

How much time and effort do you want to invest in building your business?

How much risk are you willing to take on?

What level of sales do you desire to achieve—and in what time frame?

What kind of practice do you want to build or be part of—an individual practice or part of a larger team or workgroup?

What market or niche do you want to focus on?

What brokerage firm best fits your personal and business interests and style of working?

As with any business, you need a detailed business plan. You should develop your plan based on your answers to these questions. Get feedback on your plan from people whose business smarts you respect both within and outside of the industry. If you're new to this business, make sure you enlist experienced real estate professionals (ideally those you don't compete with) to give you their perspectives.

Concurrently with building your business plan, you should be determining the kind of brokerage firm you want to work for. Your answers to the questions above should be pointing you to the best model for your ambitions and strategy.

You may be attracted to a real estate team model, for example. If so, you should be interviewing with teams to discover what they offer you in terms of your lifestyle goals, skills and compensation objectives.

If you've determined that you'd rather build your own business, your next task will be to put the processes and systems into place that will help you succeed. These include:

- Building a database of potential clients and customers.

- Developing a written marketing plan for prospecting into your target market area.

- Including in your written business plan a budget that outlines the financial resources you can afford to invest, assuming that many of these investments will not begin to pay for themselves in the short term.

- Creating a schedule that puts in writing how, where and when you will invest your time in prospecting for and servicing customers.

2. Become An Expert In Your Market Or Niche

You've chosen where you want to focus your sales energies. And you've signed on with a brokerage whose model aligns well with your defined objectives.

Your next task is to become an expert in your market. You need to complete a full analysis of your market or niche; you should study all sales and listings going back three to five years—or longer if possible. Your focus might be on a particular consumer niche—such as single women, young families, investors, or even traditional families looking for assisted-living communities. Regardless of your chosen customer category, you need to build a knowledge base on this group's particular wants and needs, along with trends on issues that might impact the kind of housing they aspire to.

To help with your marketing and sales efforts, you should develop printed materials that show the results and trends in your market or niche—be sure they can be easily scanned and emailed.

Next, compile a demographic profile of your neighborhood or targeted consumer niche and create presentation materials to share with your prospects.

You should also become an expert on the amenities surrounding your area of focus. And you should be able to communicate the differences between competing areas—a comparison study of your particular area or neighborhood versus other options.

Work with your brokerage firm to position yourself within the firm. Utilize its websites to communicate your specific expertise. Talk with other sales professionals within your firm about your knowledge and specialized focus. Make alliances!

You should milk technology for all it can do to help you grow your business. Examine the most effective channels to communicate and brand yourself as the expert in your market. Some of the ways you can do this are through Facebook, Twitter, LinkedIn, local community guides, and, of course, your website. You can brand your emails, add references to your website on your direct mail, link up with websites related to your area of expertise, and make videos discussing your expertise—the list is endless, and these are just some of the most commonly used.

Don't worry about trying to do everything all at once. Take on two or three tasks at a time, and become familiar with them on a deep level.

Then measure your results rigorously.

---

*Unfortunately, the perception is that all real estate professionals
are the same. To the extent that sales professionals communicate
that to their prospects or customers, then that sales professional
will not be able to create a higher-value experience,
for the customer or themselves.*

Michael Plowman, leader and coach
The Dan Plowman Team
River Rouge, Ontario

Today, consumers have access to most of the information that a sales
professional can have—not all, but most. They usually won't pay
for information they already have or services that seem mundane
or redundant. What consumers do value is the information that
isn't available online—information specific to their needs in areas
related not only to a particular house, but to the characteristics of
and amenities available in their targeted neighborhood and in the
surrounding area.

Consumers want to work with a professional who has specific expertise
in an area, a neighborhood, in a price range, within a specific segment
of consumers, or a type of house. Consumers are not monolithic; they
differ in their wants, needs, dreams and worries. As you've read in the
chapter on housing markets and consumers, generational differences
abound and cultural differences and requirements vary as well.

---

*Specialization has already arrived in our business.
To provide the best service requires expertise in too many areas
for one person to be able to deliver full service
in a consistently high-quality manner.*

Lyle Martin, Founder - Assist2Sell

That's the very first rule of thriving: You must become a consummate, go-to expert in your chosen market or niche.

3.   Develop Systems For Prospecting In Your Market Or Niche

You've defined your market and your expertise. Now, what's your strategy for finding customers? You should be asking yourself:

What is the best way to reach my audience? Direct mail? SEO? SEM? Phone? Door-knocking? Banner advertising? Facebook?

How and where am I going to generate my leads?

What is my budget?

What level of business can I reasonably handle?

Making use of your answers, you should develop a business plan outlining which channels or products you're going to use to communicate with prospects. Write it down, outline your budget—and what you expect to get from this investment.

Be sure to set aside the time and resources to ensure that when you get inquiries, you have the ability to respond to them quickly. According to a survey of the highest-producing teams and individual sales professionals performed for *Game Plan*, the largest reason for sales professionals' failure is their inability or refusal to establish a system for answering phones and emails.

Your prospecting should be a regular, ongoing, consistent, routine function of your business—every day.

Whatever tools or channels you use, you need to offer something concrete and uniquely valuable to your prospects. Communicate your specialty, your niche, and your particular knowledge of that area. Simply put, you must offer something compelling enough to reach through and get their attention.

*Social media will also replace email as the primary means
of online personal communication. This will drive businesses
that blend traditional business communication software
like Outlook and Lotus into that channel."*

Mark Willis, CEO - Keller Williams International Realty
Austin, Texas

The boom markets of 1995-2005 ruined many real estate sales professionals and brought significant numbers of new sales professionals into the industry. How did it ruin them? Many stopped prospecting because there was too much business chasing too few sales professionals. For experienced people who had been in the business for several years, it meant that prospecting was unnecessary—whether it was remaining in contact with past customers or reaching out to new prospects. There was just too much business with too many consumers who merely wanted someone to write the contract for them.

That was then, this is now.

*The biggest change in where our prospects will come from
over the next few years is that the majority of prospects
may not likely be 'friends and family'—the traditional
sources of business. Due to the market they are much more
likely to be first-time homebuyers, investors
or those being relocated for a job.
So your focus must be on how to prospect.*

Ben Kinney - Keller Williams Realty
Bellingham, Washington

There are a myriad of ways to prospect today. Some are old standbys, such as direct mail, yard signs and cold calling expired listings and FSBOs. Some are newer, like the use of social media tools, pay-per-click advertising on search engines, display advertising on real estate sites or the use of rating sites.

Social media is nothing more than referrals from friends and family—it's just taking on a new face in the form of Twitter and Facebook and so on. Realtors® will have to be successful in managing those relationships and networks or they're going to be in trouble, because these have become such a core part of people's DNA today.

One tool that will become more prevalent in real estate is the use of ratings of Realtors®. There have been a number of failed attempts at creating Realtor®-rating platforms. We don't know what form it's going to take in the future, but Realtors® will start getting more engaged in making sure they have ratings available. Not necessarily because consumers are demanding them, but because ambitious Realtors® will become more proactive in soliciting feedback from their clients, and search engines will do more to promote these ratings in response to real estate related searches.

No matter what strategies you choose, success in real estate will require success with lead generation. And success with lead generation requires attracting consumers upstream from the competition and having follow-up systems that help you cultivate these consumers over time. This is critical, because while historically many agents have avoided "lookie loos" and "tire kickers", successful agents today have discovered that these early stage searchers are exactly the type of prospects you can build your business around if you have the systems in place to assure rapid response, and cultivation over time. This strategy is supported by the fact that nearly 70 percent of consumers select the first agent that they interview.

To get to the front of the pack, Realtors® must promote themselves where consumers are; which is of course online. With 90 percent of consumers using the Internet as part of their search process, real estate professionals need to find ways to engage with these consumers early and there are countless options to do so. Agents can advertise on real estate web sites such as Realtor.com, Zillow, or Trulia; promote themselves on social media platforms such as Facebook, and Twitter; or, on rating sites like Yelp and Angie's List; they can buy pay-per-click advertising on search engines like Google, Bing, or Yahoo!; or, even work with companies that help manage these campaigns so agents don't have to, such as Market Leader.

In fact, there are more ways to prospect than most people have either the time or financial resources to develop fully. What has been missing from most sales professionals' tool kits is the focus on choosing one or two and getting extremely good at those channels.

Again, it's not which one you choose, it's choosing one or two, setting up systems to measure results and making adjustments based on their viability as you move forward.

4. Build Systems for Servicing Leads and Customers

In the previous section, we talked about how technology has stepped up to the plate in terms of offering sophisticated tools for lead generation. The same can be said for relationship management tools.

There's a huge selection of CRM (Customer Relationship Management) systems to choose from. You'll need technology that will automate the process of keeping track of your prospect inquiries, whether email or phone, and track your communications with them. Your software should also assist with automated responses to common questions, and calendar each prospect-related event that requires your attention.

You also need to develop a system that will identify the type of prospect who inquired, and create the appropriate methodologies for follow-ups based on the individual needs and requirements of each.

You should carefully develop a plan for how you intend to follow up with inquiries, phone calls and emails. How, when and where will you dedicate the resources to answer the phone calls and email inquiries that your prospecting system generates? What time of day, using what resources?

Apart from a failure to engage in prospecting, the greatest weakness among sales professionals is their inability, failure or refusal to follow a system for returning phone calls and emails. Studies consistently show that the majority of consumers want a response to an email in less than 30 minutes—with the allowance for phone calls a bit longer. Surveys also show that over half of all emails are unreturned after 24 hours; for our industry, the average time for the remainder of responses is more than three hours.

Many sales professionals comment that most emails and some phone calls are not related to someone interested in purchasing or selling "at this time"; they just want information. Yet few have any way to sort those who need information from those who may have at least an intermediate-term interest in buying or selling a home. And surprisingly, few sales professionals have a system in place for following up in a time frame appropriate to each particular prospect's interest.

Utilizing CRM technology effectively is not rocket science. According to the most successful sales professionals, *each and every caller or emailer is a prospect for real estate services*. Perhaps not now, and not even this year, but at some point these consumers are prospective buyers, sellers or renters. They are your target audience. Most importantly, with the right systems in place, you can manage hundreds, sometimes even thousands of such relationships. And this is exactly how top professionals generate a steady and predictable flow of business year-in and year-out.

There are numerous systems that have been built to assist real estate sales professionals in managing inquiries. These CRM systems are either desktop or web-based tools that can identify, store, respond to and calendar your prospects. The best of these systems send automatic responses and follow-ups, file information and send reminders, track activities of your prospects, and many other functions. And of course, they are integrated with your MLS, website, marketing applications, and other core systems so that you can spend your time working with clients, not copying and pasting listing or client information.

Companies like Market Leader and Top Producer have built two of the leading CRM tools specifically designed for real estate professionals and these are just two of the many options available.

Finally, there are two critical points about implementing a technology management system if you wish to thrive as a sales professional:

- First, you must have a system that is durable enough to handle the prospects your system generates. As we discussed earlier, your system should integrate easily with other systems and provide the tools you're looking for.

- Second, you must make a commitment of your personal time to follow up with prospects.

5. Build Your Brand

Building your brand is all about cultivating and communicating the unique and compelling services you provide to your customers.

Make sure you have a niche or expertise that you can own. This can be a geographic area such as a neighborhood or subdivision; a demographic group like empty-nesters; or a transaction type, such as short sales. The key is to differentiate yourself from the pack and build a steady flow of business as a result of your expertise.

You need to craft a message that clearly communicates your difference—your uniqueness. For example, it can be your experience or longevity; the size of your business; the awards you've received in your specialty; or how many homes you've successfully marketed and sold in a particular neighborhood. Most importantly, be sure to craft these messages so that they clearly communicate value to your target customer. Don't make it about you, but about what you can do for them.

Of course, your message must also be memorable. The book, *Made to Stick*[12], outlines six principles of memorability. Specifically they say that the most memorable messages are those that are: Simple, Unexpected, Concrete, Credible, Emotional, and Tell a Story. They call this their SUCCESs Model:

---

12   Chip Heath and Dan Heath, Made to Stick, Random House, 2007

Simple
Unexpected
Concrete
Credible
Emotional
Stories

This book offers great tips on how to make your messages stick—and how to make yourself top of mind for your target customers.

◆ A Brief Primer On The Meaning Of A Brand

Brand is the personality that identifies a product, service or company (name, term, sign, symbol or design, or combination of them)—and how key constituencies like your prospects, customers and clients perceive it and experience it.

People engaged in branding seek to develop or align the expectations behind what is termed "the brand experience." The point is to create the impression that a brand associated with a product or service has certain qualities or characteristics that make it special or unique. A brand is, therefore, one of the most valuable elements in advertising or marketing initiatives, as it offers a shorthand or direct way to communicate what the brand offers in the marketplace.

• Brand Awareness

Brand awareness refers to customers' abilities to recall and recognize the brand under different conditions and link the brand name, logo, qualities and so on to certain associations in memory. As a tool for helping shape customer behaviors, brand awareness helps customers immediately—and emotionally—connect with a product or service provider.

Brand awareness ensures that customers know which of their needs are satisfied by the brand through its products or services.

"Brand love" is an emerging term that encompasses the perceived value of the brand image. Brand love levels are measured through social media posts or "tweets" about a brand. "Liking" a particular brand on Facebook can also be a measurement of the level of brand love.

- Brand Promise

The marketer and owner of the brand must have a vision of what the brand must be and can do for their prospects and customers.

Brand promise is what a particular brand stands for. It has its roots in the identity that it gains over a period of time. It should go without saying that the brand's promise must be fulfilled, or brand love will plummet!

- Branding In Real Estate

Real estate brokerage firms and sales professionals talk about brand constantly, frequently without fully understanding what it takes to establish a true brand. Jack Trout, author of more than 30 books on branding and marketing over a 35-year career, questions whether real estate professionals can truly achieve a bona fide brand. As says Trout, "Brands in the residential brokerage industry are not brands in the classic sense where they describe a series of unique services and experiences, but more the sharing of a brand name with brokerage firms and sales professionals."

Trout is not saying brand names are unimportant, only that in residential real estate, they don't describe different levels of services or experiences from other real estate brands. From this perspective, in residential real estate, the existing brokerage brands, both national and local, are more powerful when viewed as a business-to-business brand, where brokerage firms and sales professionals are making decisions about whether to associate with each other. They are not meaningfully different from each other insofar as the housing consumer is concerned.

For sales professionals, there are several important points to keep in mind when setting out to attempt to establish a brand:

- No sales professional—or even sales team—is likely to have enough resources to establish a market-wide brand.

- To the extent that a sales professional can establish themselves as an expert in a certain geographic location, type of property or transaction, with a type of demographic group, or other segment, there is a great opportunity to establish a brand within that community of consumers.

The real, and very potent, power of brand for you as a sales professional is your ability to create a meaningful difference between the services and expertise you possess and that of your competitors in your chosen marketplace. These must be communicated in a way that reinforces the relevance and quality of your services and/or your expertise to your targeted consumer segment.

The messages that support the building of your brand must be compatible with what you offer and should communicate *your unique value proposition*, one that will resonate with the customer segment you pursue.

Again from Trout, "If you can't be the leader in a segment, invent a new segment." When in the process of building a brand, find a niche *where you can be the leader*. A good example might be "Sarah Jones is the No. 1 sales professional in the Briarwood subdivision" or "Bob Jones is the top real estate professional in REO property in the city."

The messages can also convey an important difference or focus, such as sales professionals who use the words "Trusted advisor to homeowners for more than 20 years." Or they can evoke a feeling, like "Find your Freedom"—the tagline for United Country Real Estate that makes an emotional connection with those seeking property in the American countryside.

Thriving in the Future

The role of the sales professional has changed in many ways over the past 10 years and it will continue to evolve in the future. As a sales professional, you are no longer simply an information gatekeeper: You are now a consultant/navigator/advocate.

In other, meaningful ways, the purpose of the sales professional has not changed greatly over time:

*The purpose of a sales professional is to help
people buy and sell homes. Regardless of how and where
a consumer makes contact, to be successful, to thrive,
sales professionals must assist people
in buying and selling homes.*

Brian Buffini, CEO - The Buffini Company
Carlsbad, California

The manner in which sales professionals can build their business has changed in the kinds of tools they make use of. But many fundamentals remain the same. These include the importance of maintaining contact with people on a constant basis and sharing your expertise with them, whether they're people you already know or those with whom you have yet to build a relationship.

Over the past 10 years, we've seen a great deal of consternation about the future for real estate sales professionals. For those who've been a part of the real estate industry for the past 30 years, a nagging worry has persisted—that some new business model or technology would render the sales professional obsolete.

But as we have discussed, the size, complexity, and infrequency of the real estate transaction coupled with the consumer's very reasonable fear of 'failure' has shielded real estate from the fate that other industries have succumbed to.   But of course, to be successful, real estate professionals have had to become more than gatekeepers of information, and have had to create value as true advisors throughout the real estate transaction.   But success with today's consumers requires more than just transactional expertise.

In a guide to top sales teams published in 2010, REAL *Trends* shared the results of research into successful sales professionals:

Leading sales professionals are focused on lead management systems and substantial marketing programs, are highly disciplined about their training, and have developed specialized approaches to growing their businesses.

- Additionally, what they found is that leading sales professionals:

- Are highly organized and disciplined

- Invest substantial time and money in systems to measure their performance across each part of their business

- Set specific goals and objectives

- Believe strongly in building their own brand exclusive of their relationship with their brokerage firm's brand

- Invest substantial time and effort in continuous training and education

Top-performing teams and sales professionals focus on:

- Outlining a clear vision for the team in terms of business objectives and culture

- Having a concrete business plan

- Establishing systems for every function of the business and for any members of a team (when they have one)

- Establishing measurement systems for all key areas of the business, not the least, how success is defined and measured

Further, their research has found that having a vision of what you want to achieve is highly important.

The key areas of defining a clear vision are:

- What do you stand for?

- How do you want to be viewed by your clients and customers?

- What are your personal goals? This should be stated not just in terms of sales volume or earnings but also in terms of personal achievement.

As everyone engaged in this business knows well, for every successful sales professional, there are far more that fail to achieve the mark they've set for themselves. What we have witnessed during this horrendous economy over the last five years is survival by focus and specialization. Your commitment to a thoughtful and disciplined approach to defining your market, and putting the systems in place to connect with that market, will serve you well. You must be diligent, smart, flexible, sensitive to your customer, and protective of your reputation. It also helps to be yourself—and to feel great about the work you're doing and the people you're serving.

Remember that people flee to quality in tough markets. Have fun, work hard, stick to your strategy or build a better one—and always keep your goals clearly in sight.

Conclusion

Much in our industry has changed in recent years while much else has remained the same. And while no one can predict the future with certainty, there are some things we would be willing to bet on, with a high degree of confidence.

First, for the foreseeable future, consumers will continue to buy and sell homes, and the vast majority of those consumers will utilize real estate professionals to help them navigate this large, complex, and infrequent transaction. If you agree, then you also know that there will continue to be significant opportunities to build profitable businesses in real estate in the years ahead.

Second, the changes we have seen in both the practice and nature of real estate will continue and will most likely accelerate in the years ahead. This means we will need to be insightful and nimble. It also means that the opportunities ahead of us will likely be even more significant than those of the past.

Third, most of the trends that will determine who will thrive, and who will not, over the next five years, are already evident in the information we have at our disposal today. At the same time, it is easy to be distracted by our past and our legacy views of the world. Those who are most successful will be those who are aware of their context, but not unnecessarily burdened by it.

Finally, each of us has the power to be successful and to reap even greater rewards than those that have come before us. There will continue to be a great opportunity for those who have the vision to see it, the courage to act on it, and the self-awareness and humility to adapt to an ever-changing environment.

We hope that you enjoyed our humble take on our industry. More importantly we hope it helps you build your own game plan for real estate success in the years ahead. Good luck and best wishes for a healthy, happy, and prosperous future.

Ian and Steve

About the Authors

Ian Morris

Ian Morris is the President and Chief Executive Officer of Market Leader (NASDAQ: LEDR), a leading provider of software and marketing solutions to the real estate industry.   Under Ian's leadership, Market Leader has grown from a cutting-edge idea into a publicly-traded company that was ranked by Deloitte and Touche as the 4th Fastest Growing Technology Company in North America.

As one of the pioneers of the online real estate industry, Ian has been helping leading real estate professionals grow their businesses for 15 years and has been named one of Realtor Magazine's Most Influential People and an Inman Innovator of the Year.

Before joining Market Leader, Ian worked at Microsoft, where he helped launch the Microsoft Network and Microsoft HomeAdvisor. Ian holds an MBA from The Harvard Business School and a BS from Bryant College.

Steve Murray

Steve Murray is editor of REAL *Trends*, the nation's leading trends and research organization for residential real estate, and president of REAL *Trends* Consulting, Inc. He has been in the residential real estate field for over 34 years.

REAL *Trends* is read by more than 24,500 leaders in the residential realty industry every week and over 500 CEO's attend REAL *Trends* conferences each year. REAL *Trends* has been a leader in industry and housing consumer research for the past 24 years. Such reports as the REAL *Trends* 500, Canadian 200, the 2006 Consumer Tsunami Study and The Wall Street Journal/REAL *Trends* The Thousand (ranking of the nation's top sales professionals and teams) are examples of REAL *Trends* research.

REAL *Trends* also publishes the REAL *Trends* Blog, which reaches over 17,000 of the nation's most productive sales professionals.

REAL *Trends* Consulting, Inc. has handled over 2,150 client assignments for realty firms over the past 24 years, with over 620 merger and acquisition assignments, totaling $10.6 billion in aggregate value. Murray has served dozens of state and local Realtor® associations and MLS organizations in a consulting capacity and several large technology firms serving the residential real estate field.

Murray manages five Executive CEO Groups composed of over 90 leading realty firm CEO's from across the country.